SENSING:
THE WAY BACK TO
NO-THING-NESS

ESSAYS ON NON-DUALITY

BENAZ SHIDFAR

Copyright Notice © 2019 by Benaz Shidfar,

Just-Isness Publications

All Rights Reserved

Book design and editing by Brianna York

Cover design by GISI Marketing Group

Cover image from Depositphotos

ISBN: 978-0-578-57487-5

Sensing: The Way Back to Nothingness

Acknowledgments

Dedication to the sages and spiritual teachers
whose words are lessening human suffering

Sri Nisargadatta Maharaj
Ramana Maharshi
J. Krishnamurti
Joel S. Goldsmith

The message of "Sensing: The Way Back to No-Thing-Ness" that is shared in this book and on the website www.just-isness.com is intended to provide information on the subject of Non-Duality. What is communicated here is not meant to be used to cure an illness, to heal the body, or as a substitute for professional advice or psychological treatment. Instead, it is intended to guide the reader to go beyond the concept of the mind and body to realize the state of No-Thing-Ness.

Who Wants to Realize Clarity When Clarity Is?
Who Wants to Be Free When Freedom Is?
Who Wants Peace When Peace Is?
Who Wants to Find Love When Love Is?
Who Wants to Realize Truth When Truth Is?

Excerpts

With the seed of sensing, a mind, body and the world appears as existence, and as the sensing becomes aware of "It-Self" as pure sensing, it dissolves and disappears. What is realized is No-Thing-Ness as the "Absolute-Being".

* * *

The individual is labeling What-Is-Happening as right or wrong, and by doing so, it is limiting the free movement of What-Is-Happening. But still, that limitation which is finite as What-Is-Happening is happening within the Infinite.

* * *

This is not a spiritual or religious message, because there is nothing outside of "It-Self" that needs to be realized or has been lost in order to be found. It is "What-Is". The No-Thing-Ness is nothing and is everything. The search for the so-called "Absolute-Being" is futile. The search is what is actually hiding the very thing that the individual is seeking for, which is No-Thing-Ness as being "All-Things".

* * *

A birth of so-called time is due to the illusion of an individual who believes to be here and the world out there. As a matter of fact, the "center" creates time to have a start and end in order to make sense of the "Time-Less", which is not of time. "Time-Less" is just the sensing of What-Is-Happening with no beginning, no middle, and no end.

* * *

An individual who thinks "This-Is-Not-It" apparently creates time and space, here and there, and this illusion of a center causes the "center" to continue its belief in separation and therefore also its belief in the necessity of searching for the truth of unity.

* * *

The ocean without movement cannot realize itself until it starts moving as the idea of an ocean. It is modified and individualized as current, then modified and individualized as waves, and then modified and individualized even more as a drop of water. These different forms of the body of water are various concepts that the ocean is seemingly forming, all happening spontaneously outside of the sea, by the ocean, and like the ocean, in the ocean and never separated from the sea. Resistance to this natural unfolding is futile.

* * *

For the sake of describing and communicating, all pointing, and naming is being used to describe God, world, mind, and body. In fact, there is no separation between these elements, but all are continuous movements of No-Thing-Ness in a most harmonious, meaningful way, that causes its colors to be in everything and at the same time being "Color-Less", "Meaning-Less", and "Substance-Less".

* * *

An individual is constantly comparing what is happening to what is supposed to happen related to different circumstances. This constant contradiction to have a better outcome than "What-Is", is the cause of the suffering of the individual. No matter if an individual is craving a desire or refusing (aversion) and resisting the outcome, it results in the need for a "me" to continue with the story for years to come. At one point in life, the individual starts its journey on the path of spirituality to desire God and resist what is not God and therefore opens the door for the separation of the "worry-center" to last, perhaps for a lifetime.

* * *

Apparently, the sensing of What-Is-Happing is receptive and responsive to its own impulses. It is well-directing, well-sustaining, and well-being because there is nothing outside of it to deny that. No-Thing-Ness is "Self-Aware," "Self-Compassionate," "All-Knowing," and "Self-Realized" to no one. It is "All-There-Is," and it forms itself like this and that and runs through all these apparent forms, revealing "It-Self" as harmony, peace, and unconditional love. It is like a light of a universal color that stands behind all colors to express their true essence.

* * *

The individual is struggling because it believes that it needs to achieve a result. The individual's substance is What-Is-Happening, which is already complete and in no need for any outcomes.

* * *

There is no right or wrong, only "Is-Ness". There is no being poor or rich; there is only "Is-Ness". There is no feeling of lack or fear, only "Is-Ness".

* * *

The image in the mirror does not exist as a real entity. Similarly, the illusion of seeing a mirage is about having a wrong perception, based on a "center" that is falsely perceiving an individual being here and the world out there. Realizing the clarity of this wrong perception allows the dissolution of an individual or "me" and the end of seeing a mirage as reality. What remains is What-Is-Happing as "All-There-Is" with no interpretation or labeling. What remains is just the "Is-Ness".

* * *

No-Thing-Ness is not withholding anything to satisfy a desire because it is "All-That-Is", fulfilled "As-It-Is".

No-Thing-Ness is not withholding to heal because it is "All-It-Is" as "Ease-Ness" and "All-Well-Ness".

* * *

The individual, as the separate-self, cannot get rid of thought because it is the thought itself. The "me" is formed by a thought that is believed to be real as an entity. Therefore, "me" cannot distance itself enough to see this truth, and from this point of view, the thought is looking to liberate itself from itself, and so it continues on the path of spirituality for years to come. When thinker and thought disappear into the thinking, what is realized is No-Thing-Ness as "All-There-Is", which is embracing everything.

* * *

A thought needs a thinker, and in the absence of a thinker as "me", the false concept of an individual dissolves with no trace as never existed.

* * *

A thought is arising, and a reaction to that thought creates a thinker, which gives an appearance of an "I" who is going to experience the cause and effect of this phenomenon as action and reaction. As long as "I" believes in being separate from its "Source", its story will continue in the field of "Time-Less" and "Space-Less".

* * *

Another meaning for liberation is embracing "All-That-Is", which is "Love" that embraces good and bad, wrong and right, dark and light, mortality and immortality, bondage and freedom, ease and disease, lack and abundance, and hate and kindness.

* * *

Where there is no "me" or a "worry-center", apparently a feeling of anger arises, and it is liberated as the sensing of What-Is-Happening as compassion.

Where there is no "me" or a "worry-center", apparently a feeling of fear arises and is liberated as the sensing of What-Is-Happening as courage.

Where there is no "me" or a "worry-center", apparently a feeling of lack arises, liberated as the sensing of What-Is-Happening as abundance.

* * *

No-Thing-Ness is unconditioned and not divided against itself, free of ignorance of separation, and therefore, with no sense of separate-self. It is the "Limit-Less" free being limited as "me". There is no beginning to its existence, and there is no end because it is "All-There-Is" as "Is Ness". It is "Self-Aware" and liberated to "It-Self", by "It-Self", in "It-Self", as "It-Self".

* * *

There is no access to the so-called physical world other than through the sensing of What-Is-Happening.

* * *

When an individual remembers an event in the past or the future, it is not actually an event that happened, but rather it is the No-Thing-Ness as the sensing of What-Is-Happening forming as sensory information/vibration of so-called thinking, remembering, or feeling; impersonal, for no one.

* * *

Before realization, conditioning such as labeling and judging, are happening all the time to allow for an individual to function. After realization and falling away of "me", "mine", and "I", the sense of separate-self still functions and continues actions such as walking, talking, thinking and turning its head in response to a name-calling, *but there is no longer an individual, or an "I", who has a relationship with "What-Is"*. It is only What-Is-Happening with no meaning or purpose, which remains only as of the "Good-Ness", the "Easi-Ness" of No-Thing-Ness as "Pure-Being". Its essence as "Love", "Kind-Ness", and "Tender-Ness", continues and apparently gives birth to a kinder, gentler mind and body toward the world.

* * *

Seeing and hearing a car passing by and knowing that it is only a projection is like seeing a body in the mirror and knowing absolutely that it is a reflection of an image. *What keeps the illusion of a body as real, is believing in thoughts that say otherwise.* Worse than thinking an image in the mirror as the real body is the belief that you can change the so-called reality (what-is) by changing its reflection in the mirror. In "Truth", there is nobody known as a body, no mirror, and therefore no reflection. It is all rather a play of light, with no purpose and no meaning other than just the sensing of What-Is-Happening as the essence of "One-Ness" that takes shapes of many different images as this and that and at the same time, not as this and that but "Pure-Being".

* * *

The essence of No-Thing-Ness is the light that shines over the so-called separated part of itself as "me" that is conditioned by the layers of fear and a sense of lack. The light of Divine shines over the shadow of ignorance of the individual in order for the "worry-center" to come out of the darkness of being a separate-self and realize itself as being part of the "Whole-Ness". Apparently, the process is called enlightenment, healing, and liberation.

* * *

Apparently, thought is arising, and the response is seemingly the natural, ordinary, and harmonious movement of No-Thing-Ness to fulfill the need around that so-called thought, with no story attached. For example, there is a thought arising with an expression of going for a walk, and spontaneous action comes in the form of getting ready to go out for a walk with no story attached around the action. In the case of "me" or an individual, the thought is arising, and there is a response to fulfill the need just as before, but apparently, a reaction takes place instead of a response. The reaction is colored and limited by stories like "I am too tired to go for a walk," or "it is cold or hot," or "my back is hurting," and therefore a feeling of stress is created by not taking the responsive action. Stress is amplified by the consequence of non-action (or action) and more reaction and drama surrounding it. The layers and layers of reactions as conditioning cover responses that could have been so natural without the story of "I" or individual, which continues to exist for some time. Liberation is the fulfillment of an apparent need by the free movement and not by the reaction that has been colored by a limitation of an illusion called "I", which is a projection of ignorance, that distorts the "Truth".

CONTENTS

.

SENSING:
THE WAY BACK TO
NO-THING-NESS

ESSAYS ON NON-DUALITY

Benaz Shidfar

CHAPTER 1

Sensing: Being "Self-Aware"

Reaction to emotion apparently arises from the deepest level of the subconscious mind as a feeling of anxiety and fear, and as it increases, consequently the emotion intensifies too through the cycle of actions and reactions. Meanwhile, the feeling of fear and anxiety is being embraced by the Self through love and compassion by the sensing of What-Is-Happening as "All-Is-Well". When there is no longer false observation to distort the sensing of What-Is-Happening by the five worldly sense perceptions and two bodily and mind sense perceptions, then there is a realization that the sensing is being aware of sensing (awareness is being aware of awareness) in its purest state. What is clearly being seen is that No-Thing-Ness, like the pulsation of God, is running through all creations as the "Sense-Less," "State-Less," and "Form-Less" through which all forms are seemingly appearing and disappearing. No-Thing-Ness is illuminating the illusion of body, mind, and the world as "It-Self," by "It-Self," to "It-Self" and back unto "It-Self".

* * * *

With the seed of sensing, a mind, body and the world appears as existence, and as the sensing becomes aware of "It-Self" as pure sensing, it dissolves and disappears. What is realized is No-Thing-Ness as the "Absolute-Being".

* * *

There is no out there, out there. Out there is apparently the projection of What-Is-Happening. Perhaps it is close enough to call it an effect rather like a hologram. There is no reality beyond the sensing of What-Is-Happening; anything else is the perception of a wrong perception.

* * *

The individual is labeling What-Is-Happening as right or wrong, and by doing so, it is limiting the free movement of What-Is-Happening. But still, that limitation which is finite as What-Is-Happening is happening within the Infinite.

* * *

This is not a spiritual or religious message, because there is nothing outside of "It-Self" that needs to be realized or has been lost in order to be found. It is "What-Is". The No-Thing-Ness is nothing and is everything. The search for the so-called "Absolute-Being" is futile. The search is what is actually hiding the very thing that the individual is seeking for, which is No-Thing-Ness as being "All-Things".

* * *

In one breath What-Is-Happening appears as:

This is not it.

This is not good enough.

I need to search in order to find it.

I am not whole.

I need to transform myself.

I need to be a better person to deserve God.

Something is wrong with me.

And in the next breath, there is a clarity that No-Thing-Ness is what is apparently arising and disappearing as this and that.

* * *

From No-Thing-Ness comes the sensing of the movement of energy, which is being "Self-Aware".

* * *

No-Thing-Ness apparently appears as the sensing of What-Is-Happening in the form of "I-Am-Ness" and on a deeper level, as the sensing of being "Self-Aware" as "I- Am" and finally "Self-Aware" merging back unto "It-Self" as "I," the "Absolute-Being".

* * *

The No-Thing-Ness is happening as the sensing of What-Is-Happening for no one.

* * *

The sensing of What-Is-Happening cannot be measured or be understood from the point of view of an individual as a separate-self. The Infinite cannot be limited or be isolated, even though at the same time, the limitation is also a form of an Infinite manifesting itself as separation.

* * *

No-Thing-Ness apparently is the sensing of What-Is-Happening and is not something out there happening to someone.

* * *

No-Thing-Ness apparently is happening as the sensing of "What-Is", not affected by anything outside of It-Self because it is "All-There-Is" and nothing is outside of it.

* * *

No-Thing-Ness is apparently happening without being a subject that has an object, and at the same time, seemingly these phenomena are appearing and disappearing into the field of No-Thing-Ness.

Seeing-Is-Happening.

Hearing-Is-Happening.

Touching-Is-Happening.

Tasting-Is-Happening.

Smelling-Is-Happening.

Thinking-Is-Happening.

Bodily-sensation-Is-Happening

* * *

It is not an individual who is shifting the perception, but rather the energetic shift happening to no one without any effect from the so-called outside world. An apple is an apple, and sadness is a sadness that apparently is happening as the sensing of seeing or touching or smelling. Therefore, there is no more identification with the apple as being red, fresh, or rotten. An apple is left alone to be just an apple, and this formulation applies to

4

everything, including the "me". There is no individual, "I," or "worry-center" with thoughts of its own. What is left to be realized is peace, unconditional love, and harmony that is sensing the essence of God being present in everything.

* * *

There is a belief that someone is living in the body which is observing, thinking, and making things happen. When the so-called individual or "I" drops away, all the beliefs about the "me" or self, fall away and the "I" stands alone in uncertainty, not being sure of its true nature. Then apparently, there is the potential to see clearly the bigger picture as "One-Ness" being Whole.

* * *

The reaction to What-Is-Happening is limiting the movement of Reality. In the field of non-duality, this gives birth to the illusion of the world of duality, where the dream of cause and effect is happening. Where there are judgments, so the expression of wrong and right doing exists, and therefore the individual or "worry-center" has to live with the consequences of its judgments as Karma, of course by no one.

* * *

There is no sound being experienced outside of the sensing of hearing.

There is no sight being experienced outside of the sensing of seeing

There is no thought being experienced outside of the sensing of thinking

There is no emotion being experienced outside of the sensing of feeling.

There is no smell being experienced outside the sensing of smelling.

There is no touch being experienced outside the sensing of touching.

There is no taste being experienced outside the sensing of tasting.

There is no bodily-sensation being experienced outside of the sensing of being.

* * *

When this impersonal No-Thing-Ness becomes personal, the story and drama are born and sometimes in this lifetime, this life-force apparently awakes to "It-Self" as "Is-Ness".

* * *

There is no infinite mind, finite mind, or higher self. There is No-Thing-Ness that apparently is the sensing of What-Is-Happening as the sensory information of sight, sound, or smell forming as seeing, hearing or smelling, of course to no one. All is as impersonal as "That".

* * *

Even the individual, "I," or "me" is "That".

* * *

The finite, infinite, or absolute are all labels that are given to "That", the No-Thing-Ness, or God, by the mind. So how can the mind understand "That"? The mind as a substance that is living in time and space cannot understand the nature of No-Thing-Ness because its movement is always in the so-called past and the future. The mind cannot get, find, seek, or search for something that is "Time-Less" and "Space-Less". The very act of wanting to understand, get, or seek apparently puts the veil over the so-called "Truth" (Truth is a label too) and at the same time, the individual is seemingly a separate-self which is not separate from the totality of the Whole.

* * *

The No-Thing-Ness apparently is the sensing of What-Is-Happening as sensory information named sound or thought, which are forming as hearing or thinking.

* * *

The essence that apparently is shared through the sensing of What-Is-Happening from the point of view of the perception of seeing, hearing, tasting, smelling, and touching, is the world perceptions and thinking and being which are the perception of the mind and body. These phenomena are appearing as No-Thing-Ness in the field of No-Thing-Ness and disappearing back into No-Thing-Ness.

* * *

The No-Thing-Ness conditions and limits the ability of the "Self" to experience something outside of "It-Self" as the so-called world.

* * *

The world is seemingly appearing in many diverse ways and at the same time, sharing the same essence that runs through all these different appearances.

* * *

No-Thing-Ness is not separate from the sensing of What-Is-Happening. No-Thing-Ness is forming as sensory information. For example, from sight comes forming of seeing, from sound comes the forming of hearing, and from touch comes the forming of touching. The seeing, touching, hearing, smelling, thinking, and being, all share the essence of No-Thing-Ness. The different movements of an ocean appear as ripples, waves, and finally, as a single drop, are appearing in various forms, and at the same time, they are all sharing the essence of the ocean. These forms which are made out of the water are the movements within the sea, and they don't exist when the ocean "Is-Not".

* * *

Perception of the World — Awake State

Sensing is not happening as the individual knows the meaning of happening. In other words, sensing is "Move-Less" and always "Self-Aware" that gives the impression of the world, similar to an awake state.

No-Thing-Ness is apparently the sensing of What-Is-Happening that is forming as sensory information or vibration called touch and appearing (which is being "Self-Aware") as touching for no one.

No-Thing-Ness is apparently the sensing of What-Is-Happening that is forming as sensory information or vibration called sight and appearing (which is "Self-Aware") as seeing for no one.

No-Thing-Ness is apparently the sensing of What-Is-Happening that is forming as sensory information or vibration called sound and appearing (which is "Self-Aware") as hearing for no one.

No-Thing-Ness is apparently the sensing of What-Is-Happening that is forming as sensory information or vibration called aroma and appearing (which is "Self-Aware") as smelling for no one.

No-Thing-Ness is apparently the sensing of What-Is-Happening that is forming as sensory information or vibration called taste and appearing (which is "Self-Aware") as tasting for no one.

Perception of the Body and Mind – State of Dreaming

Sensing is not happening as the individual knows the meaning of happening. In other words, sensing is "Move-Less" and always "Self-Aware" that gives the impression of the mind and body, similar to a state of dreaming.

No-Thing-Ness is apparently the sensing of What-Is-Happening that is forming as sensory information or vibration called bodily-sensations and appearing (which is "Self-Aware") as being for no one.

No-Thing-Ness is apparently the sensing of What-Is-Happening that is forming as sensory information or vibration called thought and appearing (which is "Self-Aware") as thinking for no one.

No-Thing-Ness – The State of Deep Sleep

Sensing is not happening as the individual knows the meaning of happening. In other words, sensing is "Move-Less" and always "Self-Aware" that gives the impression of no world, similar to a state of deep sleep.

No-Thing-Ness is self-aware as being present as the Absolute.

* * *

Apparently, the presence of the natural movement of No-Thing-Ness is the appearance of the awareness being aware.

* * *

It is not a two-part split between awareness and thought. There is not someone who is the observer, and a thought which is being observed, but instead there is the sensing of What-Is-Happening as thinking which is self-aware. For example, the seeing is the sensing that is being self-aware, or hearing is the sensing that is being self-aware. Also, there is no time between the sensing of What-Is-Happening and what is happening. There is no start or end, rather all sensory information as seeing, hearing, thinking are all happening simultaneously, and it is only a matter of the contraction or constraint would be an indication of where the so-called manifestation "Is".

* * *

What-Is-Happening is not changing because there is no before and after. Therefore, there is only this as "That", only this as "That", only this as "That", only this as "That". It is What-Is-Happening, but not in time and therefore not in the Now as we know it. Now is not a time, but it does represent the essence of What-Is-Happening.

* * *

A liberated free movement of a vibration proceeds to become thought, then thinking and then the mind, which projects the perception of the world. Any reaction to any so-called state makes this natural process personal, which has to be experienced by the self who is living in a world of duality.

* * *

Who wants to realize "Truth" when "Truth" IS?
Who wants to realize clarity when clarity IS?
Who wants to find freedom when freedom IS?
Who wants peace when peace IS?
Who wants healing when well-being IS?
Who wants to have wealth when abundance IS?
Who wants to find love when love IS?

Who wants to find fulfillment when the fulfillment IS?
Who wants to get wise when wisdom IS?

* * *

The game of the hide and seek continues as long as an individual or "I" believes in separation from its source of No-Thing-Ness. There is no more illusion or a dream of a separate-self when No-Thing-Ness is realized.

* * *

It is this sensing of a separate-self that is manifesting its false existence as the individual.

* * *

The "I" is "That" too, but apparently the individual appears in a very extreme contradiction to What-Is-Happening with the sense of separate-self as "I".

* * *

It is not that the "Form-Less" is taking a form to manifest itself as someone who is begging and praying for its realization, it is instead the free movement of "Is-Ness" that appears to no one and disappears back unto "It-Self", all spontaneously as the sensing of "What-Is".

* * *

There is no "Time," and there is no "Now". There is instead What-Is-Happening apparently arising as a thought, a feeling, a sight, or a sound by no one to no one. Reacting to What-Is-Happening manifests "I" because the reaction comes from an individual who believes in being here and that the world is out there.

* * *

A birth of so-called time is due to the illusion of an individual who believes to be here and the world out there. As a matter of fact, the "center" creates time to have a start and end in order to make sense of the "Time-Less", which is not of time. "Time-Less" is just the sensing of What-Is-Happening with no beginning, no middle, and no end.

* * *

Maybe there is a truth to Karma but only in relation to an "I". The individual, which believes in right and wrong, manifests the sensing of its judgment as good and bad into its reality. This reaction is often named Karma to life experience. Meanwhile, an individual and its judgments as yin and yang are part of the Whole and also the movement of No-Thing-Ness that is happening for no one and to no one.

* * *

There is no "me," "I," or an individual that was born and is going to die. There is no mind or body that was born and is going to die. These are all concepts that the separate-self has created to deal with the challenges of being separate from "Death-Less" and "Time-Less". "All-Is" is No-Thing-Ness as "Time-Less," which gives the appearance or concept of birth to this moment and as "Death-Less" which gives the impression or idea of death to this moment.

* * *

The feeling of fear is the same as love, but it is labeled and judged by the separate-self or "me".

dis-ease is the same as "Ease", but it is labeled and judged by the separate-self or "me".

* * *

When an individual stops naming experiences, No-Thing-Ness is realized as a thought in relation to a mind and bodily-sensation in relation to a body.

* * *

Emotions are arising as the feelings of anxiety, sadness, anger, and can even manifest as the feeling of bliss and happiness, private and personal in relationship to an individual. Framing and labeling through believing in separate-self is what creates a reaction to What-Is-Happening (which is impersonal) and creates the "center" that eventually starts reacting to emotion (which is impersonal) and forms the feeling of suffering.

* * *

There is nothing outside of emotions to make them personal. It is an impersonal phenomenon appearing and disappearing as What-Is-Happening.

* * *

An individual who thinks "This-Is-Not-It" apparently creates time and space, here and there, and this illusion of a center causes the "center" to continue its belief in separation and therefore also its belief in the necessity of searching for the truth of unity.

* * *

The "I", which is known, cannot know "Un-Known".

The "I", which is limited, cannot know "Un-Limited".

The "I", which is filled with conditioning, cannot know "Empty-Ness".

The realized "I" cannot know "Un-Realized".

The "I", which its movement is in the past, and the future cannot know "Time-Less".

The "I", which is divided, cannot know "Un-Divided".

The "I", which is from time and space cannot know the "Un-Movable".

* * *

Going to work, being retired, raising kids, traveling, seeking, being religious, being spiritual, being single, being in a relationship, all are happening with no one claiming the ownership of doing as the doer. As soon as the individual is making this natural movement of No-Thing-Ness personal, the separation from its "Source" becomes its reality, and so too it's suffering.

* * *

A separate-self from its position can only understand something that has a place or a location. Therefore, the No-Thing-Ness that is without a center is hidden from an individual point of view when the self is acting as a seeker.

* * *

The individual has no place to ask why because What-Is-Happening has no cause, no effect, and therefore no individuality to ask questions. It is "What-Is".

* * *

No-Thing-Ness as "All-There-Is" cannot wake up to non-duality because there is nothing outside of itself that knows about duality. It is what it is, as it is. It is liberated and also not liberated

* * *

No-Thing-Ness is nothing and is forming as everything.

* * *

"Infinity" as "All-Ness" is becoming finite and therefore forming as something.

* * *

An object such as a cup does not exist, and it is the manifestation of its vibration, interpreted by the so-called observer into an illusion of something named a cup.

* * *

The ocean without movement cannot realize itself until it starts moving as the idea of an ocean. It is modified and individualized as current, then modified and individualized as waves, and then modified and individualized even more as a drop of water. These different forms of the body of water are various concepts that the ocean is seemingly forming, all happening spontaneously outside of the sea, by the ocean, and like the ocean, in the ocean and never separated from the sea. Resistance to this natural unfolding is futile.

* * *

There are no waves, but instead, there is a rising and falling of what is happening as the so-called ocean. Similarly, there is nobody, but instead, there is seemingly a rising and falling of the sensing of What-Is-Happening as bodily-sensation, forming the concept of a body.

Compare this to the saying "don't judge the book by its cover". Similarly, specifying or framing the sensing of What-Is-Happening that is forming as a body and calling it beautiful or ugly, is false. A body is just the sensing of bodily-sensation as "What-Is," which cannot be named.

* * *

No-Thing-Ness has movement as pure energy, which is called love, compassion, peace, ease, happiness, and harmony. What distorts and therefore puts this absolutely pure vibration behind a veil, is a reaction which is part of

No-Thing-Ness and not separate from it. As long as this apparent body and life are called "my body" and "my life," reaction and therefore, distortion is happening until it is not.

* * *

No-Thing-Ness is not called "One" because then there would be a perception of seeking the "One". In non-duality, it is called "Not-Two" or "One undivided without a second" to stop seeking God as one entity separate from the seeker.

* * *

For the sake of describing and communicating, all pointing, and naming is being used to describe God, world, mind, and body. In fact, there is no separation between these elements, but all are continuous movements of No-Thing-Ness in a most harmonious, meaningful way, that causes its colors to be in everything and at the same time being "Color-Less," and "Meaning-Less".

* * *

From No-Thing-Ness, seemingly the world appears. And in No-Thing-Ness seemingly, the so-called world disappears, leaving a slight footprint of the sensing of What-Is-Happening for no one to no one as "Absolute-Being".

* * *

No-Thing-Ness is the essence of everything, even the so-called illusion or mirage of this apparent world, with no separation. Its being in the most authentic nature is "Is-Ness".

* * *

An individual is constantly comparing what is happening to what is supposed to happen related to different circumstances. This constant contradiction to have a better outcome than "What-Is", is the cause of the suffering of the individual. No matter if an individual is craving a desire or refusing (aversion) and resisting the outcome, it results in the need for a "me" to continue with the story for years to come. At one point in life, the individual starts its journey on the path of spirituality to desire God and resist what is not God and therefore opens the door for the separation of the "worry-center" to last, perhaps for a lifetime.

* * *

There is nothing spiritual in the practice of breathing, meditation, or mindfulness. These are just apparent movements that seemingly disconnect the constant distortions that are caused by so-called thinking, which is the habit of the chattering mind and connect the meditator with the sensing of What-Is-Happening.

* * *

When there is no more "me" or a need for the individual, there is instead the constant sensing of appreciation for the wonders that are unfolding for no one.

* * *

The appearance of "I" is like a lucid dream. One-day, an individual wakes up, and there is a realization that there never was a "me" or "mine". Instead, all there is, is "In-Visible," "Un-Nameable," and so very intimate as the Self.

* * *

Thinking is happening as the movement of No-Thing-Ness, which is self-aware.

Bodily-sensation is happening as the movement of No-Thing-Ness, which is self-aware.

Being aware as the awareness is happening as the movement of No-Thing-Ness, which is self-aware.

* * *

When there is no individual, therefore there is no reaction, all that remains is "This", as the peace that transcends all understating.

* * *

The sensing of What-Is-Happening that is forming as sensory information of sight and sound has no objective qualities or forms but is being ever-present, and at the same time, "I" or "worry-center" disregards this truth and believes in the illusion that is called the physical world.

* * *

The sensing of what is happening is all there is in relationship to What-Is-Happening, and it is not an event that is happening independent of everything else in the apparently physical world.

* * *

The individual is apparently working hard to get rich, get healthy, gain clarity, and get free in order to live a happy life. Meanwhile, what "I" is desperately trying to reach is already What-Is-Happing for no one.

* * *

Apparently, the sensing of What-Is-Happing is receptive and responsive to its own impulses. It is well-directing, well-sustaining, and well-being because there is nothing outside of it to deny that. No-Thing-Ness is "Self-Aware," "Self Compassionate," "All-Knowing," and "Self-Realized" to no one. It is "All-There-Is," and it forms itself like this and that and runs through all these apparent forms, revealing "It-Self" as harmony, peace, and unconditional love. It is like a light of a universal color that stands behind all colors to express their true essence.

* * *

Thought that has been conditioned by believing the self to be separate from its source, forms itself as "me" and apparently manifests its own suffering, while all along the "me" is "All-That-Is" as No-Thing-Ness.

* * *

Knowing that there is such a thing as so-called sin, is keeping the "Truth" at a distance while being aware shines a light on the act of sin as What-Is-Happening for no one.

* * *

The sensing of What-Is-Happening is not a state which an individual can get in and out of, rather No-Thing-Ness as the sensing of What-Is-Happening is continuous without any distortion or interruption. Being continuous with no interruption is apparently called peace, which has passed all understanding. Realizing this truth is liberation.

* * *

The thought is not an appearance standing alone by itself but is What-Is-Happing labeled as thought.

* * *

No amount of effort or suffering could change the outcome because there is no outcome to be changed. Getting rich or getting healthy is like wanting to change an image in the mirror. It is useless. Being happy, peaceful, and healthy is the movement of What-Is-Happening, and the concept of "trying" actually creates separation from the "Source" of its "Being" which is peace and well-being.

* * *

The individual is struggling because it believes that it needs to achieve a result. The individual's substance is What-Is-Happening, which is already complete and in no need for any outcomes.

* * *

While there is no out there external to the self, such as a world or an individual who is living with fear and feelings of loss, What-Is-Happening appears as the reflection of "All-That-Is" and not separate from "All-That-Is" as love and richness for no one and to no one.

* * *

Apparently, the limited and finite mind which reflects and projects a body with the feelings of lack and fear is not separate from What-Is-Happening. In the time of realization, the so-called finite mind is dissolving back into the "Mind-Of-God" as What-Is-Happening and what is realized is the sensing of love, compassion, and well-being.

* * *

Apparently, the finite-mind as a separate entity is the extension or instrument that "Infinite-Mind" of God as

"It-Self" is using to project itself in the form of the world, mind, and the body on the screen of No-Thing-Ness.

* * *

The essence of No-Thing-Ness is the light that shines over the so-called separated part of "It-Self" as "me" which is conditioned by the layers of the feelings of fear and loss, and illuminated in order for the individual to realize itself as part of "Whole-Ness". Apparently, the process is called enlightenment, healing, and liberation.

* * *

An individual's desire is based on the duality of being a "center" which is seemingly operating from here, and it is craving to change the world. "All-That-Is" is What-Is-Happening that is illuminating the illuminator and illumination and it is content already with no desire as its nature is already fulfilled.

* * *

No-Thing-Ness apparently is the sensing being self-aware of What-Is-Happening, as the sensory information named sound, which is appearing in the form of hearing for no one.

No-Thing-Ness apparently is the sensing being self-aware of What-Is-Happening, as the sensory information named sight, which is appearing in the form of seeing for no one.

No-Thing-Ness apparently is the sensing being self-aware of What-Is-Happening, as the sensory information named thought, which is appearing in the form of thinking for no one.

* * *

No-Thing-Ness as "One-Essence" is the sensing of What-Is-Happening, appearing in various forms (formulations or modulations of original forms), similarly to the ocean that appears as multiple forms, from the current to a wave, to a drop of water, all sharing the essence of water.

* * *

The essence of "One-Ness" is like the light of the sun that shines over just and unjust alike because it is not separate from "It-Self" while embracing "ALL".

* * *

The essence of No-Thing-Ness is the "Is-Ness" as "All-Ness," therefore its nature is illuminated as love, abundance, wholeness, peace, harmony, and joy. Its movement is fulfilled as "It-Self," by "It-Self," through "It-Self," and back unto "It-Self".

* * *

Conceiving, receiving, perceiving, experiencing, and expressing are all appearances of No-Thing-Ness as What-Is-Happening as "It-Self," by "It-Self' and back unto "It-Self".

* * *

There is no right or wrong, only "Is-Ness". There is no being poor or rich; there is only "Is-Ness". There is no feeling of lack or fear, only "Is-Ness".

* * *

A "center" is the individual, and its reaction to What-Is-Happening is the cause of its distortion. This distortion is the same as the belief that an individual accepts as the truth that keeps the "me" in the dark shadow of separation

* * *

Feelings such as lack, fear, anger, and shame are arising apparently from believing that there is a being as a separate-self called an individual.

* * *

The "Invisible" is the "Source" that apparently projects itself as the sensing of What-Is-Happening in the form of the individual. It starts from "Absolute-Being," then becomes the sensing of What-Is-Happening as the sense of peace, harmony, and love. Last it will change back to No-Thing-Ness.

* * *

Apparently, death is the end of the arising of those particular thoughts, feelings, and perceptions and not the end of No-Thing-Ness.

* * *

The image in the mirror does not exist as a real entity. Similarly, the illusion of seeing a mirage is about having a wrong perception, based on a "center" that is falsely perceiving an individual being here and the world out there. Realizing the clarity of this wrong perception allows the dissolution of an individual or "me" and the end of seeing a mirage as reality. What remains is What-Is-Happing as "All-There-Is" with no interpretation or labeling. What remains is just the "Is-Ness".

* * *

From the point of view of an individual, a mirage which is based on misperception is falsely seen as being a real event. Similarly, the same individual that is believing in deep-rooted feelings of lack and fear is wrongly living in a world of illusion.

* * *

When the illusion of duality is dissolved within, apparently the outer mirage disappears, and what remains is "All-There-Is" as "One-Ness".

* * *

There is no cause behind seeing, thinking, feeling, and hearing; instead, it is just "Is-Ness" that is appearing as What-Is-Happening in many forms.

* * *

There is a metaphor that explains this model. No-Thing-Ness is the light that illuminates every frame, which is the sensing of What-Is-Happening as displayed by the projector. The projector projects the content of each frame of "What-Is" back on the screen of No-Thing-Ness. There is no separate individual acting as a character in the movie; therefore, no actor, and no action. There is only acting as No-Thing-Ness, by No-Thing-Ness, and back unto No-Thing-Ness. There are apparently different forms that are being illuminated by No-Thing-Ness as the sensing of What-Is-Happening, which are projected on God's Mind without any external reality. Seemingly, it is all a dream taking place in Divine Mind.

* * *

No-Thing-Ness is the essence that runs through the sensing of What-Is-Happening as thinking, being, seeing, hearing, and touching. The essence of No-Thing-Ness is love that is not excluding anything and is embracing "All-That-Is". Love is the glue of existence that runs through life, embracing the feelings of lack and fear that resides in the individual or "worry-center". "Worry-center" is having these feelings because they are based on and shaped from a sense of separation. The individual or "worry center" is love. It cannot separate itself from love, but "I," believing its being is separate from its "Source," is resisting "What-Is" and continues with its search for the "Truth".

* * *

No-Thing-Ness is the perceived, perceiving and perceiver. No-Thing-Ness is "Self-Aware," and its nature is:

Omnipresence as being "All-There-Is".

Omniscience as being "All-Sensing" ("All-Knowing").

Omnipotent as being "All-Mighty-One".

* * *

There is no limitation or conditioning. They are all different forms of God's appearances. There is a reaction that creates a sense of separation, and as a result, the "worry-me" is born.

* * *

No-Thing-Ness has movement in the existence of itself and is not in need of a so-called object such as an individual to become aware or to know "It-Self". It is "Self-Aware" of its own existence or movements.

* * *

Being an observer to seek and find the "Truth" is what veils the "Truth".

* * *

Apparently, every mind and body has its own unique pattern and layers of conditioning which are being illuminated by the light of No-Thing-Ness as Uni-Verse (the metrical rhythm of the song). No-Thing-ness is expressing "It-Self" as love, compassion, kindness, harmony, peace, and vitality. These expressions are illuminated by the light of No-Thing-Ness and could be metaphorically compared to a drop of water, wave, or inner current in the ocean. All these changeable forms come apparently to existence from the point of view of No-Thing-Ness, which is "Un-Moveable," "Un-Changeable," and "Un-Avoidable" because there is only the Divine.

* * *

No-Thing-Ness is the sensing (knowing that is self-aware) of What-Is-Happening in various formulations and dimensions which comes as the results of its appearing and disappearing, effortlessly and spontaneously without any prior motivations or impulses. It could be called a dream in the mind of God.

* * *

No-Thing-Ness is without Karma, and it is its own cause and effect because there is nothing outside of it to become an effect.

* * *

While witnessing or observing is as What-Is-Happening; what is perceived, witnessed, and observed are all the various forms of No-Thing-Ness.

* * *

Love is to embrace all, and grace exists to pull everything to itself, all as the power of God at work.

* * *

The intention is about turning our head within ourselves, and grace is about keeping the attention within until "Absolute-Love" is realized.

* * *

Apparently, in the last state, the entirety of sensing dissolves spontaneously into No-Thing-Ness and what remains is "Absolute-Being".

* * *

No-Thing-Ness is the sensing of What-Is-Happening as sensory information of sight, touch, sound, smell, taste, bodily-sensation, and thought. These seven elements are forming and appearing as touching, hearing, smelling, tasting, being, and thinking. The emotion which is the subtle vibration of existence is being intensified by reactions that are caused by beliefs, memory, and limited conditioning, and therefore, feelings are being felt at the level of mind, body, and the world perception as the feeling of fear and loss. These intense emotions are being experienced by the individual and therefore, the reincarnation of these forceful emotions will continue appearing in the next moment called Now.

* * *

There would be no sense of separation if there is no more reaction which means the "I" or individual is dissolved, and love which is the essence of No-Thing-Ness as subtlest emotion is being sensed in its purest form in the Now as the sensing being "Self-Aware".

* * *

Emotions are intensified by reactions on the level of the subconscious mind. These reactions are caused by identification with a mind and body. These intensified emotions are felt as feelings such as anger or hate by an individual who believes themselves to have these feelings. When the individual dissolves, what is left is the pure essence of What-Is-Happening in the form of love, peace, and compassion, which runs through all experiences for no one. For example, the bodily-sensation called back pain, which is What-Is-Happening is continued by way of identification to the body, and therefore neutral emotions are now being intensified and being sensed (felt) as the feelings of anxiety, anger, and despair. As a reaction to pain becomes less and less, the emotions return to their neutral state and are sensed as their true essence of No-Thing-Ness, which is the sensing of "Well-Being". This process is called healing.

* * *

The neutral emotions are intensified to reactions (at the subconscious level) by the arising of seeing, touching, hearing, smelling, tasting, thinking, and being. These apparently heightened emotions are now called feelings and have reincarnated themselves every moment and become personalized feelings in a relationship with an individual. They are therefore being sensed (felt) as the feelings which an individual feels such as anger or sadness. Reincarnation is the label that is given to the next emotion and therefore feeling, that manifests itself as the personal feeling of an individual.

* * *

World perception is about sound, sight, taste, touch, and taste, which are forming as hearing, seeing, smelling, touching, and tasting as What-Is-Happening. Body perception is about bodily-sensation forming as being and mind is about thought to form as thinking. The effect of world sense perceptions and body-mind sense perceptions on neutral emotions are feelings which are being sensed and felt on the level of mind and body as the feeling of happiness or sadness. The sensing of neutral and impersonal emotions as the pure essence is the next subtle level, and the sensing of being aware of sensing (being self-aware) is the deepest level of sensing; the quickest way to the realization of "One-Ness".

* * *

An individual might be feeling anger or jealousy, but a sense of compassion and kindness is there to embrace those feelings that are part of the story of "me". The feeling is more related to a situation or an event on the level of the mind, body, and world, nevertheless, the sensing, which is self-aware, is the more subtle and more profound element that embraces all kinds of feelings such as anger, anxiety, depression, and excitement as love and compassion.

* * *

There is no solid body which on the inside is feeling pain, but the feeling of anxiety or hate is what is happening and could be sensed on a deeper level by the subtlest vibration as the sensing of "All-Is-Well".

* * *

There is no actual body which has an inside and outside with different organs. Instead, it is the vibrational instrument vibrating at different levels which manifests itself as a "center" and a world as being out-there, all from the mysterious and magical way of naming and labeling. As a matter of fact, the body is No-Thing-Ness, which is the sensing of What-Is-Happening as bodily-sensation.

* * *

The body is apparently the projection of the sensing of What-Is-Happening.

The mind is apparently the projection of the sensing of What-Is-Happening.

The world is apparently the projection of the sensing of What-Is-Happening.

* * *

The essence of God (No-Thing-Ness) is Love.

* * *

It is not even true that What-Is-Happening is appearing as touching, hearing, smelling, tasting, seeing, thinking, and being. Instead, it is the sensing of "What-Is" that is being sensed which manifests the mind, body and the world. When there is no reference to call a body, mind, or world, what is realized is the sensing that is self-aware of being "Self-Aware", "Knowing" that is self-aware of being "Self-Aware", or "Awareness" that is self-aware of being "Self-Aware" as the Divine.

* * *

There is nothing outside of the sensing of "What-Is" that is being sensed. What is being sensed as the sensation is not an object separate from the sensing. There are still the sensations sensing themselves. So, there is no individual hand as a body part independent of being sensed. Apparently, everything is arising, forming, appearing, and from nothing and goes back to nothing. The body is not independent of the color that seemingly sees or independent of bodily-sensation that is being felt, and so it is also not independent of sensing of itself and likewise not independent of its source as No-Thing-Ness, or the Divine. What is being sensed is illuminated by the light of No-Thing-Ness as What-Is-Happening, projected on the screen of No-Thing-Ness, apparently to be experienced by no one and turns back into No-Thing-Ness as the end of its life cycle.

* * *

Sensing is not apart from sensation and therefore at its core sensation itself, is being "Self-Aware".

* * *

What-Is-Happening is a pure sensation. Any labeling, judgment, or reaction towards it gives an appearance of the sense of separation. For example, pain is the bodily-sensation that is as What-Is-Happening, but any judgment and therefore reaction towards it with regards to how bad it is, or how tense it is, gives an appearance of an individual who is having the pain and thus also experiences the feeling of anxiety and suffering. This is true with all other feelings that manifest the belief in a separate-self.

* * *

No-Thing-Ness is the sensing of What-Is-Happening as the bodily-sensation that, at its core, is the pure essence of well-being.

No-Thing-Ness is the sensing of What-Is-Happening as the thought-sensation that, at its core, is the pure essence of loving thinking.

No-Thing-Ness is the sensing of What-Is-Happening as the sound-sensation that, at its core, is the pure essence of joyful listening.

No-Thing-Ness is the sensing of What-Is-Happening as the sight-sensation that, at its core, is the pure essence of blissful seeing.

No-Thing-Ness is the sensing of What-Is-Happening as the taste-sensation that, at its core, is the pure essence of the celestial taste.

No-Thing-Ness is the sensing of What-Is-Happening as the touch-sensation that, at its core, is the pure essence of healing touch.

No-Thing-Ness is the sensing of What-Is-Happening as smell-sensation that in the deepest and purest essence is a heavenly aroma.

* * *

There is no individual who is realizing No-Thing-Ness. Apparently, abiding in the sensing, which is self-aware, is an ultimate practice in itself. This means that total-rest and total-surrender in sensing is the total liberation from the perception of the world, mind, and body. The next state is when the "center," or the individual disappears into the sensing of itself, and at last, the sensing disappears into "Essence-of-Love". All that remains is the sensing that is being aware of the sensing, knowing that is being aware of knowing or awareness that is being aware of being aware. In the last state, sensing which is self-aware is abiding in "It-Self," by "It-Self," as "It-Self," in its purest essence of love and merges into No-Thing-Ness. When the sensing of seeing is love and sensing of touching is love, and sensing of thinking is love, then liberation is realized by the grace of Divine.

* * *

Sensing that is self-aware of "It-Self" as its purest essence merges into No-Thing-Ness and realizes itself as being "All-There-Is".

* * *

The meaning of surrendering is seemingly surrendering all desires and wills to the will of God. This includes even the desire for liberation. This means leaving all the responsibilities to God as the "One" who causes these desires to appear and for whom fulfillment happens, and then they all disappear into No-Thing-Ness as if nothing happened.

* * *

Life-Force is the movement of the essence of No-Thing-Ness as love, peace, and harmony, which apparently is manifested through coming into contact with the five world sense perceptions and two mind and body sense perceptions. This manifestation relating to its "Source," has the essence of non-duality as love, and when it is distorted and disconnected from its origin, then it appears as the belief of separation and duality. Meanwhile, at any given time, it is the "Source" itself and not separate from itself.

* * *

Seemingly, on the one hand, sensing is the sensing of What-Is-Happening as changeable and on the other hand, is the sensing of No-Thing-Ness as "Un-Changeable".

Seemingly, on the one hand, sensing is the sensing of What-Is-Happening as the feeling of hate, and on the other hand, is No-Thing-Ness as the sensing of the "Compassionate-One".

Seemingly, on the one hand, sensing is the sensing of What-Is-Happening as the feeling of anxiety and on the other hand, is No-Thing-Ness as the sensing of "Kind-Ness".

* * *

The sensing is not a feeling itself. It is instead sensing of the feeling. Sensing and the sensor and what is being sensed are all various forms of No-Thing-Ness or the Divine.

* * *

No-Thing-Ness is changeable and movable that is forming as this and that which creates "All-Ness," and at the same time, No-Thing-Ness is unchangeable and immovable as not-this and not-that being "Nothing-Ness".

* * *

Only No-Thing-Ness embraces "ALL-There-Is".

* * *

No-Thing-Ness is not love, but love is arising in No-Thing-Ness as the unconditional essence of No-Thing-Ness.

* * *

No-Thing-Ness is void of any essence as "Essence-Less," and void of time as "Time-Less" and void of a boundary as "Bound-Less". Nevertheless, its subtlest, slightest movement at its first pulsation is arising and forming as sensing, and the projection of its essence is the essence of "Unconditional-Love".

* * *

When there is no longer an individual with a sense of separation or desire for something that is different from What-Is-Happening, then the push and pull subside, and reaction and identification with the body lessens. At that time, the sensing of What-Is-Happening diverts its attention to the sensing of the essence of No-Thing-Ness, which is unconditional love, and which eventually is sucked by grace into No-Thing-Ness and remains as "Absolute-Being".

* * *

Feelings of anger, sadness, and fear are indications that there is a distance between an individual who is sad, the feeling of sorrow, and the situation that caused the grief. The truth is that all of these phenomena are happening spontaneously. The only thing apparently separating the individual from the feeling is the labeling and therefore, the judgment. Otherwise, these various appearances are all arising and subsiding in No-Thing-Ness as sensing of What-Is-Happening. As the realization arises that what is realized as the world is actually a five-sense perception and that the two mind and body sense perceptions are not separate from itself as "It-Self", then what remains is the illumination of the pure essence of the unconditional love as No-Thing-Ness, the Divine.

* * *

The mind and body are just labels. In fact, they are the so-called sensing instruments (sensory) that are sensing "It-Self" as what is being sensed. When the sensor, sensing, and what is being sensed dissolve in non-duality, what is realized is the "One-Ness" of "All-There-Is".

* * *

No-Thing-Ness is the "State-Less" state, the "Empty-Ness" that the sensing of What-Is-Happening is arising from to give birth to the existence or not arising from to end existence.

* * *

No-Thing-Ness is embracing thoughts, feelings, and sensations to harmonize them to its own frequency of unconditional love, similar to the waves of the ocean, which continuously go back to the shore to claim what it has left behind.

* * *

Whatever is conceived in the mind of God is projected on the screen of No-Thing-Ness in order to be sensed by no individual but the Divine.

* * *

No-Thing-Ness is like a sun that is shining at all the time, even if the inside of the house is dark. The metaphor can be applied using the window as the means to the sensing of What-Is-Happening. The more we open the window, the more sunlight can get in. At the same time, we can say this about the sensing of What-Is-Happening. As an individual becomes more colorless, the more light of No-Thing-Ness is realized. Therefore, the deeper the practice gets, the more realization of God there is. Not to mention that the individual who practices and what is being practiced and practicing are all the same. They are just various forms of God appearing as this and that. Like the sun and its ray of sunlight and the miracles of shining are all the same.

* * *

Apparently, without the acceptance of pain and embracing the feeling of suffering, the individual or "me" is living in a vicious cycle of action and reaction, which triggers the cause and effect. The cycle has been called Karma. By embracing pain, the sensing of "Well-Being" and "All-Is Well" is realized on a deeper level.

* * *

Sensing is "Self-Aware". Seemingly, on the surface level, the separate-self feels the feeling. The sensing of the feeling is done below the radar of negative or even positive beliefs, limiting conditions, and the storehouse of memories of the past and worries of future events. Therefore, the sensing is embracing the feeling of What-Is-Happening on all kind of levels, from the reactive state to the non-reactive. As sensing becomes more subtle and more refined, it senses the essence of No-Thing-Ness as pure, unconditional love.

* * *

In the last state, sensing is being aware of itself as "It-Self," which is the path to the realization of No-Thing-Ness.

* * *

Emotions are the movements of life-force and the activities of "Is-Ness" or No-Thing-Ness, which are giving form to the arising and subsiding of What-Is-Happening. Sensing, which is being self-aware, becomes the manifestation of No-Thing-Ness when it starts pulsing, which means it comes into existence. When the sensing of What-Is-Happening is arising as impersonal emotion, the world comes into existence, and as it is subsiding, the world goes out of existence.

* * *

The feeling is the reaction (the feeling is a reaction to the flow of life-force) to the emotion at the subconscious level by the so-called mind, which gives birth or manifests more intensified emotion as the feeling of suffering or anxiety. Reaction to emotion manifests the sense of separation that is called an individual or separate-self or "me". This is the vicious cycle of Maya (for Maya's definition please refer to Q/A section), but the truth of a matter is that at all times, it is No-Thing-Ness as What-Is-Happening and not a moment separate from "That". As the false concept of mind and body drops away, so is reaction weakened, and the feeling of suffering softens. The sensing becomes more subtle and becomes more notable until sensing, which is being self-aware, is sensing the essence of No-Thing-Ness as pure unconditional love. Apparently, in the next state, as grace arises, the sensing that is being aware is abiding in the state of "Non-State" as "Un-Movable," "Time-Less," "Matter-Less," "Change-Less," and "Bound-Less" as "Absolute-Being". Without any sensation as the results of the dissolution of body and mind, then VOID "Is" as eternal potential.

* * *

Sensing appears and disappears in No-thing-Ness. The sensing is the ripple of first or subtlest movement of No-Thing-Ness as pure unconditional love. As emotion intensifies to the reaction of the sub-conscious mind, then it is named or labeled as the personal feeling of an individual as the feeling of anger or happiness.

* * *

Emotion, when intensified, becomes feeling, and feeling is further reinforced by the reaction from the sub-conscious mind. They are all different names for the same "Source" they are arising from and subsiding to.

* * *

38

Sensing appears and disappears in the No-Thing-Ness. When it appears, sensing is the essence of No-Thing-ness as unconditional love, and when it disappears, VOID "Is", which is eternal potential.

* * *

To make this clear, the sensing is running through all the different apparent stages and appearances. Sensing of unconditional love embraces the feeling of What-is-Happening, such as the feeling of anger or anxiety. Also, No-Thing-Ness is not something that the individual can abide within, so everything permanently is part of No-Thing-Ness, including the "me" or the "worry-center". The individual gets stuck on the path of spirituality, believing that being an observer or someone who is being aware is the way to realization. No-Thing-Ness is "Just-Isness". That is all. It is not a container or a field that something is arising from. It arises as itself, by itself, and returns to itself. As long as there is any kind of movement, such as life-force, then there is sensing to be sensed. Another way to say this is that sensing is being aware of the sensing, which is not separate from God, and it is God that is "Self-Aware". Divine's nature is Omnipotent, Omnipresent, and Omniscient, and when there is no movement, GOD is void of any activities.

* * *

There is a doer or an individual who is seeking enlightenment. The way back to the realization of No-Thing-Ness is sensing of devotion, which is longing for reality, and the sensing of liberation, which is a determination for freedom, and the sensing of earnestness and unconditional love for the Absolute. Sensing is the way back to No-Thing-Ness.

* * *

Sensing is self-aware of appearing and disappearing of what can be called life-force as emotions. As the sensing becomes pure in its purest form without any distortion from false-self, then it becomes aware of "It-Self" as No-Thing-Ness.

* * *

When ignorance is seen in the light of profound understanding, the false perception of separate-self being separate from its source falls away, and apparently sensing, which no longer is distorted, is realized to be the path to God.

* * *

When the sensing is being aware of the sensing (being "Self-Aware"), which means sensing is being aware of sensing as God, then seeking is over, so is the concept of "me", and "Bound-Less," "Immense-Less," and "Change-Less" is realized by no one. The sensing that is being aware of the sensing is the most authentic reality because it is the subtlest form that is closest to the truth of God, and it ends or is dissolved with realization. Misperception about this truth and distortion towards the vibration of sensing of What-Is-Happening is the reason for confusion and therefore suffering.

* * *

Sensing of I AM THAT I AM is the end of seeking. When "I" realizes that there is no individual, fear, and desire, which are the grossest form of vibrations which are on the level of mind and body fall away, and self is realized as the "Self".

* * *

When the sensing of What-Is-Happening is the sensing of unification and devotion, then the path is paved for realization.

* * *

One layer deeper below the sensing of What-Is-Happening, where the push and pull of the separate-self or the "worry-center" comes in to play; there is a field or state of no more reacting. What is realized is the sensing of the essence of the heart of No-Thing-Ness as pure unconditional love and peace that passes all understanding. And when the sensing is being aware of the sensing, which is the final state, the self realizes itself as "It-Self," the "Un-Limited", "Change-Less", and "Time-Less". So apparently, the development is from No-Thing-Ness (I) to light (I-AM) as sensing, and to the apparent world of (I -AM-NESS) as What-Is-Happening which is illuminated by the light of the Divine. The process of Neti Neti (neither this, nor that) which is returning back from the form or an image (I-AM-NESS) to the sensing (I-AM) as light and then returning back to No-Thing-Ness as the "Source" of everything and at the end, becomes void of everything as VOID, the eternal potential.

* * *

The sensing of the essence of love does not mean that there is an individual who loves someone; rather, there is just "Loving" that is being aware of "Loving". Better said, all there is, is love as "Love-Is".

* * *

The individual's mind and body are not quiet or silent enough to sense the sensing of What-Is-Happening, but rather sensing is being felt as personalized feeling at the surface of action and reaction. Sensing is at such a core and deep level that "I", or the "worry-center" has no access to those kinds of sensations, which is very subtle for the chattering mind and restless body to sense. The feeling is what an individual can feel because this can be felt at the level of mind and body and not on a deeper level as the sensing. The deepest essence that can be sensed even in the most horrifying situations is love, which is the fundamental building block of existence when an individual is not. The closest path to the realization of No-Thing-Ness is unconditional love in its many forms. Such as:

The sensation of hearing only appears as a sound of love.

The sensation of seeing only appears as the sight of love.

The sensation of touching only appears as a touch of love.

The sensation of smelling only appears as the smell of love.

The sensation of tasting only appears as a taste of love.

The sensation of thinking only appears as a thought of love.

The sensation of bodily-sensation only appears as being in love.

* * *

There is order and harmony in the movement of No-Thing-Ness as it is spontaneously arising and falling. It is called Universal Law. Impersonal thoughts and desires are arising, then are followed by deeds and being fulfilled, and then all disappear. They are called miracles because nothing is hidden from the Divine because Divine is Omnipresent, Omnipotent, and Omniscient.

* * *

By the use of the five world sense perceptions and two body and mind sense perceptions, life-force gives birth to forms by arising and falling in which What-Is-Happening comes to apparent manifestation as the illusion of world, mind, and body and disappears back to its "Source" where everything comes from.

* * *

Sensing is the language of the inner world and the substance of creation. With the sensing, the creator is creating its creation as tasting, seeing, touching, hearing, smelling, thinking, and being, while at the same time, the sensing is being aware of sensing as No-Thing-Ness, which lies within the field of spontaneity as "All-Are-Happening".

* * *

An individual might be having a feeling of frustration or pleasure. Feeling is the reaction to What-Is-Happening on the level of the subconscious mind, but the sensing which is being aware of the feeling is at a much deeper level, without being disturbed by any events or circumstances that are apparently happening in the inner or outer world. The sensing that is being self-aware is a hidden phenomenon, deep within, with no cause and effect, which is in-tune with the essence of God. The feeling arises based on a reaction to the outer world while sensing is the essence of No-Thing-Ness, no matter what is going on in the external world. The feeling is riding over the essence of love if the individual is willing to go deep enough to observe and discover this element of the truth. At the beginning of practice, sensing is hidden or veiled by strong feelings such as anger or jealousy, but as the mind and body quiet down, the sensing of pure unconditional love which is one attribute of No-Thing-Ness is realized as love. This essence of "Absolute-Being" is always there, but it is obscured by the reactions of the subconscious mind.

* * *

The sensing dissolves as the result of the body dissolution and what remains is VOID as eternal potential.

CHAPTER 2

Healing from the Concept of Mind and Body

When there is no reaction to fear as it is arising, No-Thing-Ness, which is self-aware, remedies the distortion that is caused by fear and brings about healing for no one as "Pure-love".

When there is no reaction to lack as it is arising, No-Thing-Ness, which is self-aware, remedies the distortion that is caused by the lack to bring about healing for no one as "Rich-Ness".

When there is no reaction to disease as it is arising, No-Thing-Ness, which is self-aware, remedies the distortion that is caused by uneasiness to bring about healing for no one as "Easi-Ness".

* * *

Healing is metaphorically the acting of peeling off labels that are given to conditions of mind and body such as disease to allow for well-being to "Be". There are not two states, dis-ease, and ease, but just "Just-Isness" as the "State-Less".

* * *

An individual who is seeking health is apparently the cause of the halting of the process of healing of the so-called mind and body.

* * *

To heal humanity as a whole is for every individual to liberate itself from the bondage of conditioning as this isolated "I", separate from the "Source". The deep understanding and realization that the individual, or "I", is not different from its "Source" is true healing.

* * *

The state of an individual, or "I", is a contraction. Its nature is unease, and its world is the reflection of this state of un-easiness and is stressed. When the dis-alignment falls away, the body accordingly responds to that alignment as so-called healing. When full alignment apparently happens, there is no longer cause and effect; therefore, no ease or dis-ease or bad or good. What is being realized is that liberation and freedom are as What-Is-Happening and make way for the realization that there never was a separation.

* * *

When there is a reaction to What-Is-Happening, the appearance of the solid body may change by the vitality of What-Is-Happening. One moment it might appear as dis-ease and another moment as ease. The process is so-called spontaneous healing.

* * *

Whatever arises in the so-called body-mind as dis-ease, is going to be met and healed by the sense of well-being by no one.

* * *

When there is no lack and fear, well-being "Is".

* * *

In the field of No-Thing-Ness, whatever is being introduced will be attuned. This means that whatever that is not in alignment with "What-Is" will come into alignment with "What-Is". Apparently, the process is called healing, from dis-ease to ease, which is the attunement with well-being as No-Thing-Ness.

* * *

When a thought arises regarding the body that it is sick, with no judgment or reaction to the pain, the sensation attunes itself with "Source" to heal itself.

* * *

The unconditional sense of What-Is-Happening has no preferences between ease or dis-ease. The act of embracing all is apparently the process of healing.

* * *

No-Thing-Ness cannot know about dis-ease in order to have a desire to heal itself because its essence is unconditional. This means it is ease and dis-ease and also that it is beyond ease and dis-ease as the "Cause-Less".

* * *

There is no process that is called healing of the body other than the apparent bodily-sensation coming into alignment with the essence of No-Thing-Ness. By understanding the true nature of dis-ease, the nature of an individual, and realizing the pure essence and reality of

No-Thing-Ness as well-being allows for healing to happen.

* * *

It is not about the health of a physical body, but it is instead about the sense of well-being that already exists as What-Is-Happening, which is seemingly projecting itself as health in the so-called physical mind and body.

* * *

There is no truth in getting well other than realizing the sense of well-being seemingly projecting and revealing itself as a condition called health in a so-called physical mind and body.

* * *

There is no healing in the future but the realization of What-Is-Happing as the fulfillment of the so-called need of this moment to heal as different forms of "Is-Ness".

* * *

Even wanting to get well indicates a trace of a condition or an expectation of something out of itself that an individual is searching for in order to feel better. No-Thing-Ness is "All-There-Is," and resistance is "Point-Less," and acceptance "Is".

* * *

Healing could be spontaneous because the process of healing does not need time as well-being "Is".

* * *

When an individual realizes that "me," "I," or "mine" are all projections of What-Is-Happening and not reality, the harmony is restored as the liveliness that is called life-force to no one. With this realization, the so-called mind and body are healed from the sense of uneasiness, restlessness, and agitation to perfect health.

* * *

Apparently, coming into alignment with What-Is-Happening, which is the sense of well-being, is a form of healing.

* * *

There is an individual who wants to get well, but apparently, by realizing its "True-Essene", the "worry-center" sees beyond the illusion of this mind and body, having no root or substance.

* * *

Pain is just a sensation being labeled as "my-pain" by thought and followed by a belief of getting worse, which causes a feeling of anxiety and fear; and therefore, a sense of suffering.

* * *

The essence of God as "Being-All-There-Is" has the healing power and any desire that comes from the viewpoint of duality disturbs its nature which results in non-duality.

* * *

When healing from dis-ease apparently is needed, "Ease-Ness" appears.

* * *

Healing is not a process separate from the healer and the so-called healed person; instead, it is What-Is-Happening. When "All-Is-Well" or "Well-Being" is realized, then apparently the person who needs the healing is healed not in time but in "Time-Less" as "Time-Less" through the "Time-Less".

* * *

A thinker is not a healer, but the sensor is. The purest vibration of sensing as love is the closest vibration to the sense of No-Thing-Ness as "Well-Being", which has a power of healing for no one.

CHAPTER 3

Individual with the Sense of Separation as "I"

At the time that the individual seemingly goes to sleep, the dream world seems so real until "I" wakes up and realizes that it was just a dream. So, it is that by the time that the individual wakes up from its sense of separation, it is to realize that "me" was never separated. This is called freedom and liberation from duality.

* * *

The world and what is happening in the world are just an illusion, and when individual beliefs, which are based on the feelings of lack and fear are limited, its reaction to

What-Is-Happening is going to be limited too, which indeed sustains the existence of a separate-self as a seeker. Meanwhile, what is being formed as an individual is still the appearing and disappearing of What-Is-Happening for no one.

* * *

The individual or "worry-center" thinks it is an entity who is making decisions, but apparently, when "me" wakes up from a dream; it realizes that there was no "me" to decide. It is the same with this reality that is called life. There is no individual who is making a decision to drive a car, instead driving to the beach happens and there is a thought that is arising after the action taken to take the ownership of what has happened. That is why the activities of "I" which are in time and space are always about condemning or regret the past or worrying about the future and they are always colored by judgments.

* * *

The activities that are arising from an individual as a separate-self has apparently created impressions of cause and effect. The nature of "me" is based on separation, and so are its beliefs, which are based on the feelings of lack and fear. The individual believes something is lost, and it needs to find it. This push and pull apparently creates more of the same thing, therefore resulting in more seeking and more feeling of emptiness. The "I" is not going to realize the truth of this in order to fill the gap of separation because its true nature is separation. The play of something is lost, and what "me" has to find will never end because nothing is missing.

* * *

Any intention by the individual to get somewhere or do something in order to find happiness outside of itself apparently creates a "center" and, therefore, a world of cause and effect. It is only the individual that cares about how the outcome should be because What-Is-Happening is not good enough, and "me" or the "worry-center" has to get somewhere or something in the future in order to satisfy the need of being happy. This search will continue as the story of "I" who is living a drama called "my life".

* * *

The individual is living in a bubble of illusion as long as it is commenting on or judging what happened in the past and is worrying about what is going to happen in the future, and not in the truth of What-Is-Happening in this very moment.

* * *

No-Thing-Ness is apparently running through all the forms, arising and subsiding as the sensing of What-Is-Happening and also appearing as the limited appearance of "It-Self" by way of mind, body and the world with no apparent reason.

* * *

There is no meaning to What-Is-Happening. It does not have any agenda, no purpose, no start, and no end. Apparently, it is free-flowing and happening to no one. Its essence is free from any agendas. It is What-Is-Happening, like the flow of the stream into the ocean and not at any time separate from its totality. It embraces everything because of its nature is "All-That-Is", and that includes all. How can it separate itself? It is arising as a concept of the separate-self which is part of the stream as "it-Self". Any of its movement is "That". Any of its questionings is "That". Any of its arising and falling is "That". Any of its forgetting and its remembering is "That". Any of its searching is "That". Any of its story of being lost and being found is "That".

* * *

No-Thing-Ness embraces all because it is "All-There-Is" with no separation. Apparently, we call this notion of embracing and welcoming, the act of love and then confuse this sensing of love which is its nature with an individual who has a passion for something or someone.

* * *

The essence of No-Thing-Ness is free and liberated from any limitations and can be realized in no time, but an individual believing in separation and resistance to What-Is-Happing creates bondage and starts seeking its freedom in the field of captivity. Therefore, a seeker is born in the pursuit of freedom and happiness. An Individual starts its quest by meditating, purifying, or going through a transformation while all along, what the seeker is seeking is happening every moment as What-Is-Happening. This is obviously hidden because of the false concept of seeking. The "Truth" is so apparent that the individual believing in separation will never find the "Truth", and the game of hiding and seeking will continue.

* * *

Any movement of wanting to find the "Truth" is seeking, which is based on a sense of separation. The "me" or the individual, hides its true nature, which is based on separation by pretending to be spiritual and being on the path of non-duality to enlightenment just to find out after twenty, thirty, or forty years that the seeking is still going on. The search of the "worry-center" is the movement of separation, and its nature is to deny the very thing that it is looking for. The "me," or Individual does not want What-Is-Happening. It is the last thing the individual wants because its belief is based on "This is not it" or it cannot be so simple or obvious. The truth that the individual is looking for is the experience that is out of this world, and it should be a life-shattering experience. "Truth" is simple, ordinary, and obvious, and apparently, the silent mind realizes "That".

* * *

The "me" has dedicated its lifetime in search of the truth, believing the "Truth" is not easy to realize and takes a long time to find. The individual who wants to find happiness feels betrayed if all its effort to find the "Truth" is going to be for nothing. The individual believes its story has to have a most significant, happy ending, and it cannot end with its own dissolution.

* * *

The story of "me," is to survive its existence, and the thought of its own dissolution in order to find the obvious "Truth" is the last thing on its mind. With an individual as a separate-self, apparently comes the world of duality, the world of cause and effect, and there is no place for the truth of non-duality.

* * *

In the world of non-duality, there is nothing outside of "It-Self" to cause anything else, so it is "Non-Causal".

* * *

The seeking mind wants liberation, but it cannot liberate itself. Freedom "Is", and when the individual sees through the veil that apparently is separating itself from the "Source," then the sense of "me" as a "center" falls away by the realization of the "Truth" and become aware of its non-existence as being "Self-Aware".

* * *

The individual as an entity does not get liberated by the concept of finding the "Truth" because there is no "me" to become liberated. Realizing what is already "Limit-Less" and "Space-Less" is liberation. Even in the moment of clarity, a thought arises and claims the enlightenment which one more time hides the Divine from the seeker who thinks it has found the "Truth".

* * *

At the end of the so-called search, all that remains is, apparently What-Is-Happening – even the sense of separation is happening as "That". Talking about non-duality is as What-Is-Happening and not talking about non-duality is as What-Is-Happening. Meditation is What-Is-Happening without a concept called a meditator and drinking a glass of water is What-Is-Happening without a concept called a doer. There is "One-Thing" that is happening as "All-There-Is," and it is happening until it is not. Its movement does not have any purpose or meaning and has no beginning or end. Its nature is happening and at the same time non-happening in no time as "Time-Less".

* * *

When the seeking for the "Truth" exhaust itself, then what is in its purest form is "Just-isness," as the "Absolute-Being".

* * *

No-Thing-Ness appears as the sensing of What-Is-Happening, which is being "Self-Aware" labeled as God, which is "Omnipresent," "Omniscient," and "Omnipotent".

* * *

The individual as a separate-self cannot sense the sensing of What-Is-Happening, which is "Bound-Less" and "Empty-Ness" because of the process of naming or framing distort or obscures "It". The reason is, as soon as "me" labels or judges in order to understand or to make the sense of "It", the illusion of subject and object is created by the law of cause and effect, and this limited version of What-Is-Happening must be experienced by the seeker as the feeling of being separated from its "Source" in the world duality.

* * *

Apparently, one day, the sense of separation liberates itself from the illusion of separation, and all that remains is "No-thing".

* * *

The so-called intention is seemingly happening by the seeker who wants to understand, to control, and to create, but it is only What-Is-Happening. There is no "I" who is intending, understanding, or creating, but rather, it is just What-Is-Happening or better said the sensing of What-Is-Happening.

* * *

What is called a body is apparently No-Thing-Ness seemingly arising and being labeled as bodily-sensation and is projected "It-Self" out-there as a solid body on the screen of No-Thing-Ness. Apparently, the process of naming, labeling, or framing makes the movement limited, and therefore, the sense of separation as the concept of the individual is created. In fact, nothing is being separated from something else. It is all "Not-Two-Ness" happening and not happening at the same time. Apparently, What-Is-Happening is not What-Is-Happening because there is no reality to its existence outside of "It-Self" because of being all there is.

* * *

When there is an individual with the false belief of being here as a subject and the solid world being out-there as an object falls away, then the concept of subject and object falls away, and so does the individual at its center.

* * *

An individual's nature is all about setting a goal and expecting an outcome that creates a sense of contradictions with its own activities. In this field of inconsistency and uneasiness, apparently, the individual cannot understand the nature of "Is-Ness" that is "Un-Limited", "Empty-Ness", and "Meaning-Less". No-Thing-Ness is complete and free from its own activities. Therefore, it is free from having any outcomes.

* * *

As soon as an individual or "me" is born, there is a "center" created as the subject, and therefore, the world of cause and effect is manifested for the individual to suffer through.

* * *

A thought arises, results in a judgment, and turns something that is so impersonal as What-Is-Happening to become personal. No-Thing-Ness is apparently What-Is-Happening in the form of the sensing of hearing as the appearance of hearing and being heard, which is impersonal in the field of non-duality. It is the result of the reaction and labeling that the world of duality is apparently manifested and is being lived by the "I".

* * *

We could try to have analytical answers to all the questions in life to satisfy the needs of the mind and body to feel secure especially around the concept of death, but there is always one more question in need of an answer to fulfill this gap of separation. This gap can never be filled by the mind unless the gap is realized as its true nature and to be dissolving back into the No-Thing-Ness. Birth and death are a natural part of What-Is-Happening with no complication that needs to be talked about or solved. Every moment is happening as the birth and death of that moment as What-Is-Happening. This is a simple act that is happening by the "Effort-Less".

* * *

Like What-Is-Happening, eating is happening, so too, the feeling of anxiety is happening because of believing in the feelings of lack and fear. This feeling of anxiety is being labeled and judged by the individual who is looking for a state of happiness with no anxiety. When the individual or "me" falls away, what remains is everything as "Ease-Ness" free from the "worry-center", whose fundamental nature is uneasy and unhappy.

* * *

The individual is not going to get enlightenment or to become enlightened. Surrendering to What-Is-Happening is the gateway to enlightenment or to use another name for it, to No-Thing-Ness which individual is not.

* * *

No-Thing-Ness is self-aware, and it does not need an individual to find it because there is nothing outside of "It-Self" to find. The No-Thing-Ness is "All-There-Is" and cannot have, get, or find a piece of "It-Self" because it is its own totality.

* * *

In the pursuit of happiness, the individual or "me", whose nature is a contradiction, puts the veil on the very thing that it is searching for. But searching for the truth is the story that the individual needs to believe in order to continue within its search for something that has never been lost. The outward journey of finding God becomes the life purpose and meaning that an individual needs to have in order to continue its drama of searching for years to come.

* * *

The seeking for fulfillment is what sustains the process of looking in order to fill the gap of unfulfillment. This search gives life purpose to the "I" as an individual who loves to have a purpose in whatever it does in order to continue its existence.

* * *

The sense of separate-self thinks that he or she is the driver of the car, but the irony is that there is no car, no driver, and nowhere to drive to. There is only a journey as What-Is-Happening by no one and to no one.

* * *

It is not true that the individual is on the path of spirituality to find its true nature. The process of so-called realization is so natural and simple, but the fear of the "Un-Known" keeps the attachment in place and, therefore also, the story and drama surrounding "me".

* * *

"What-Is-Happening" is the projection of No-Thing-Ness, which appears as individualized forms of everything in the world. "I-Am" is the sensing of No-Thing-Ness that is the projector that gives substance to everything in the world, and "I" is the VOID, which is void of "All-There-Is".

* * *

Sensory information is arising as touch and is forming as touching, which is What-Is-Happening as the touching and being touched.

Sensory information is arising as aroma and is forming as smelling, which is What-Is-Happening as the smelling and being smelled.

Sensory information is arising as sound and is forming as hearing, which is What-Is-Happening as the hearing and being heard.

Sensory information is arising as sight and is forming as seeing, which is What-Is-Happening as the seeing and being seen.

Sensory information is arising as taste and is forming as tasting, which is What-Is-Happening as the tasting and being tasted.

Sensory information is arising as bodily-sensation and is forming as being, which is What-Is-Happening as being felt.

Sensory information is arising as thought and is forming as thinking, which is What-Is-Happening as the thinking and as being reflected upon.

* * *

What drives an individual's existence is a search for something better than what happened in the past and what is going to happen in the future, but never this moment, "As-Is". Its seeking is for the pursuit of happiness, health, a loving partner, and wealth which give hopes to the "me" to continue while knowing deep in its core that by realizing its true nature, the seeking ends, and also the seeker dissolves back into No-Thing-Ness.

* * *

Believing in fear and lack in the heart of the individual is what creates uneasiness, worries, and a sense of separation from its "Source". The individual which is living with these feelings for years seemingly establishes more and more the illusion of isolation, separation, and the sense of uncertainty, confusion, and the firm belief to survive. The truth of the matter is that surviving is What-Is-Happening for no one, and when this "Truth" is deeply realized, peace and harmony that have always been, there are realized by no one.

* * *

There is enough conditioning of the individual by external elements that when an individual is being called, apparently, the individual turns and answers. There is seemingly enough conditioning left for the apparent mind and body to function in the world, while "All-Is-Happening" for no individual.

* * *

Reaction to the movement of What-Is-Happening is the cause for the next escalation, which leaves the effect of the previous action-reaction to be experienced by the "center" of the individual as a continuous event.

* * *

The end of an individual life feels like a real death to the ego, because it knows there would be no hope to search for happiness. Hopefulness is what keeps the ego alive to seek for something that has never been lost.

* * *

The seeking starts when What-Is-Happening is not good enough for an individual. A seeker is looking for a better experience, so it reacts to What-Is-Happening because it wants less of that which is called aversion, or more of that which is called craving. This means that by the law of cause and effect more of what has been rejected and less of what has been craved is manifested for the individual to experience. The process of push and pull and reaction to that is called Karma, which is for that individual to experience because of its own ignorance. It is the end of resistance and suffering for the individual when "me" understands there is no right or wrong as What-Is-Happening, which is nameless, label-less, and meaningless, and there is no "I" to give it any meaning.

What-Is-Happening is what is happening by no one and to no one.

* * *

There is not something called an individual's life, because there is no separate "I" to live in it or own it. It is just the free movement of the sensing of What-Is-Happening. It cannot be owned to make it better. It is what it is as it is just happening. It is No-Thing-Ness as "Is-Ness", and the "Absolute-Being".

* * *

I want to be healthy; I want to be wealthy; I want to have a partner. All are the projections of No-Thing-Ness on the screen of No-Thing-Ness, which are being played like a movie that is being illuminated by the light of No-Thing-Ness. There is no "I" to search for a thing or to own things. Searching and seeking for something other than loving "What-Is", is futile.

* * *

When sensitivity sets in, it becomes evident that "me" constantly denies the goodness of this moment for a better experience. There is a realization that desiring for a better experience is the very substance that is hiding the goodness that the individual is searching for. At the same time, there is a realization that even seeking for a better experience is the movement of No-Thing-Ness as the sensing of What-Is-Happening.

* * *

Even desiring to realize God is the cause of separation.

* * *

After the falling away of an individual or "I", there is a realization that there was no separation, to begin with, and so-called everything is allowed to be "As-It-Is", as ordinary and extraordinary as What-Is-Happening.

* * *

When the "center", which apparently creates the illusion of here and there, is dissolved, all remains is just "Is-Ness" and on a deeper level, the "Absolute-Being".

* * *

Seeker, which at its core is contradiction and distortion, wants to find, to get, or to understand the state of no-contraction or distortion. By chasing liberation, the individual as a spiritual seeker, being on the path of spirituality, is creating more distortion and bondage for years to come.

* * *

As long as the seeker has a hidden agenda for finding the "Absolute", such as gaining abundance, healing power, or control, the "Absolute" is going to be hidden in the game of lost and found, a game that is being played by the "Absolute" , the "One" and the "Only".

* * *

The so-called "I," or the individual, is unmanifested as the pure potential that can be realized as the "One" and get liberated in no time as "Time-Less". But it takes time for this realization to happen, because of the story that "me" has created based on its beliefs and memories. As long as "I" believes in the mind and time, body and space, and the world of the duality of here and there, it is going to take time for this momentum to be stopped, reversed, and dismantled.

* * *

An individual who is looking for harmony is causing a lack of harmony, balance, and peace. Otherwise, the so-called hearing, thinking, seeing, and feeling are the sensing of What-Is-Happening, which is part of harmonious experiences that are appearing and disappearing as What-Is-Happening without an "I".

* * *

The continuous search for the "Truth" is the root cause of suffering.

* * *

The movements of push and pull apparently are caused by a desire for pleasure and also a wish to avoid the pain which causes suffering. When there is no longer craving and aversion, then what is realized is the sensing of What-Is-Happening as an impersonal form of joy and harmony to no one.

* * *

When so-called liberation happens, then there is a realization or clear sensing that there is no individual who is doing the searching; rather, What-Is-Happening is happening as searching and liberating.

* * *

What an individual is searching for is what is already appearing as What-Is-Happening, and resistance to it is futile.

* * *

The "I", or individual, is practicing the act of abiding in the hope of finding the "One" ends the search but abiding or searching is a different name for seeking, as subtle as it is.

* * *

After the so-called shadow of separate-self as an individual falls away, what remains is the sensing of What-Is-Happening being "Self-Aware" as the light of No-Thing-Ness.

* * *

The individual is an appearance too.

* * *

The movement of pulling and pushing that comes from an individual who is desiring pleasure and resisting pain is the cause of suffering.

* * *

The individual as a separate-self is seeking to find something that the "me" cannot get away from because nothing is lost. The so-called "I", or "me", is seemingly appearing as "That" and cannot be separated from "That".

* * *

An individual, or "I", cannot stay in darkness for long because its nature is light.

* * *

The so-called tensions or conditions in the body are called beliefs.

* * *

Being in a state of no desire, no will, no striving, and no hope seems like an end of the individual which, in a way, is the death of "me". When the "I", or individual, wakes up from the dream of separation, all that remains is liberation and freedom for no one.

* * *

The individual cannot love unconditionally in order to be happy because its energy is conditioned and limited based on the feeling of lack and fear. For a while, the "I" or individual, is finding happiness in the apparent world of duality that does not last for long. Eventually, not being able to find true contentment and harmony, the search for the "Truth" starts and so also does the dismantling process, which ends the illusion of separation and dissolution of a concept called an individual.

* * *

There is no Individual that is doing the seeking. There is no "me", no "mine", no "I". Existence is not about the "I" and its story. It is impersonal, no matter how much the "I" wants this so-called reality to be all about its own story. When the extraordinary personal story of the individual becomes ordinary and impersonal, then the "Extra-Ordinary" will shine through nothing.

* * *

The separate-self as a "center" has a position that is not real. It is justifying its search for the "Truth" by labeling What-Is-Happening as not being "That" and continues with its search for the Divine. At the same, the detachment and dismantling process that is again part of the story of seeking is at work. After the falling away of the concept of being separate, all that remains is What-Is-Happening, apparently liberated from purpose and free from the limitation of an "I".

* * *

An individual or "I" cannot get or find happiness, because its nature is not pleased with "What-Is".

An individual or "I" cannot get or find peace, because its nature is not at ease with "What-Is".

An individual or "I" cannot get or find fulfillment, because its nature is not satisfied with "What-Is".

An individual or "I" cannot get or find health, because its nature is always in a fight with "What-Is".

An individual or "I" cannot get or find joy, because its nature is not content with "What-Is".

* * *

When the sense of separation is dissolved, what remains is "What-Is" being "Un-Disturbed", "At-Ease", "At-Peace", "Full-Filled", and "Joy-Full".

* * *

An individual who has a "center", which constantly projects time and space cannot be present in order to be here and now. The "me" is living in a drama of the past and with anxiety for the future, which causes struggle and more suffering. What-Is-Happening is happening in the now moment, and its nature is fresh and renewed, an experience that the individual has no understanding of.

* * *

As soon as a false sense of separation has been believed as the "Truth", so begins the process of conditioning, limitation, and stress. All are limitations that are added on top of What-Is-Happening and hide the nature of "That", which is No-Thing-Ness.

* * *

Apparently, the journey of separate-self is like a wave of the ocean traveling between the shore of "I got it" and "I lost it". It is a journey with no reality because there is no wave and no ocean. "Got it" and "lost it" is just What-Is-Happening in no specific time or place.

* * *

Seeking is the last thing an individual is going to let go of. The "me" cannot justify years of seeking to be in vain. To be on the path of spirituality is what the seeker's life is all about, and so too becomes its existence is all about.

* * *

When an "I" falls away, so does its story. There is a realization that the individual had no significance, and the "me" never happened. The "worry-center" disappears, and what appears is the ordinary by way of the "Extra-Ordinary" as nothing and as everything.

* * *

Story of "me" or the individual unfolds as it is seeking the "Truth" while doing meditation, fasting, seeking, reading, abiding, being an observer, knowing, inquiry, being aware, not being aware, or letting go. All these actions continue until there is the self-realization of No-Thing-Ness.

* * *

The nature of an individual, or "me", is based on the feeling of lack and fear, and its reaction is the cause of craving and aversion. The movement of liking and disliking are the push and pull against What-Is-Happening. These reactions are appearing and disappearing in waveforms and give a sense of separation, which is based on ignorance of who and what individual truly "Is".

* * *

As it is mentioned before, the sense of separation of an individual is formed and believed in because of not knowing (ignorance) of its real true essence as No-Thing-Ness. Therefore, the nature of the individual is reactive because of having the belief of being separated from its true nature. Based on its reactive nature, the individual responses to What-Is-Happening are always judgmental and are labeled as good or bad and, consequently, cannot be happy with "What-Is".

* * *

The individual's reaction as craving and aversion manifests the push and pull, which cause distortion and alteration of the "Truth", which manifests itself as suffering. The essence of the "I" is all about desiring pleasure (based on the beliefs and memories of past experiences) and staying away from pain and suffering (based on the beliefs and memories of past experiences). When finally, reaction to What-Is-Happening stops, there would be no momentum or energy for the story to continue. Jealousy or anger is rising, and without any reaction, they will both pass, and what will be realized is No-Thing-Ness in which all the phenomena are appearing and disappearing. As a result of this realization, the individual disappears (not that it was an entity to begin with), and apparently, the so-called state of bliss, peace, harmony, and unconditional love is realized, which is NOT affected by the apparent world.

* * *

No-Thing-Ness apparently arises, and with it seemingly arises the sense of separate-self, which is part of the Whole, just to subside back unto "It-Self" with no purpose.

* * *

Because of ignorance or belief in separation, the movements of push and pull, or craving and aversion against What-Is-Happening formulate or form a sense of separation. This belief of being separate from the "Source" veils the "Truth" from the seeker and causes the seeking of the "Truth" to continue.

* * *

Tension and reaction, which are formed by the push and pull are what the so-called body is formed of. Judging, and therefore personalizing, the impersonal "One" is the process through which the "I", or an individual is born. The "I" lives in time and space in order to continually try to make sense of something that is "Meaning-Less" which is spontaneously appearing and disappearing in and as No-Thing-Ness.

* * *

"I" is the essence of No-Thing-Ness, but apparently layers of conditioning that are happening in place of being an individual makes the "me" believe that it is separate from its "Source". With this false understanding comes a sense of dissatisfaction, pain, and suffering, which on a deeper level which raises from the feelings of lack and fear. These feelings make the existence of the individual or the "worry-center" more real. Therefore, the world becomes a reflection of the very individual who needs to have power and control in order to struggle to survive. The life of "I" becomes its reflection and protection of its own limited beliefs and conditioning to continue.

* * *

To find the missing piece of the puzzle in order to be happy and fulfilled, an individual justifies its struggle, always waiting for something better to happen, which would be more satisfying compared to What-Is-

Happening. The profound belief that something is wrong at the deepest layers of the sub-conscious mind gives existence to the intolerable feeling of pain and suffering as trauma and motivation for the induvial to continue trying to fill the gap with no remedy in hand.

* * *

An individual sustains the appearance of itself by being an object here and the appearance of the world-out-there and living this false story for years. From impersonal non-duality comes "One-Ness" with no attribute, but an individual believes that there is a personal God out-there that is almighty and needs to be discovered. "Me" believes that God is going to help the individual to have more power and more control in order to provide the "worry-enter" with more security. Its relationship with personal God is all based on needs, wants, selfishness, and begging.

* * *

From the so-called moment of separation, the "I" starts seeking in order to find its way back to where it came from. The individual goes outside of itself in the world of duality to find non-duality. Its search for peace and joy takes the "me" to different relationships, jobs, religion, and adventures, but nothing is filling the gap of duality, and so the search and therefore veiling as well, will go on.

* * *

Nothing apparently is going to soothe the pain of the illusion of separation until "I" realizes its true nature, which is the essence of No-Thing-Ness. The individual continues to do what it is doing until there is a deep understating and realization that nothing is going to take away the suffering of separation until the "center" realizes itself as the "Self". Then the individual surrenders to What-Is-Happening, and with it comes the realization of liberation and freedom that "I" as the "center" seemingly has been looking for. In the moment of realization, there is an absolute knowing/sensing that the individual never was separated, and the seeking was to find itself as "It-Self".

* * *

As the illusion of separation falls away, so too does its tension. The result is an absolute pure knowing that separate-self, or "I", did not exist as an individual. The momentum of believing and trying to find God starts to dismantle and, consequently, the concept of the so-called world. The reactions to situations and problems dissolve, and as a result, so too the pain and suffering. Without "I" as a separate-self, No-Thing-Ness that is limited by no one shines as "Whole-Ness", "Full-Ness", and "Complete-Ness". It is no longer life is being lived in a world of duality which is defined by the law of cause and effect but effortlessly as "All-There-Is"

* * *

No-Thing-Ness has no start, no end, no meaning, no purpose, and is not coming from anywhere, and not going to anywhere. It is without intention because it is "All-There-Is". There is nothing missing that needs to be found because there is nothing out outside of "It-Self". It is liberated and free as inner peace, joy, well-being, harmony, and unconditional love. It is "Self-Aware" and by being "It-Self," as "It-Self" and back unto "It-Self", exists as a pure "Absolute-Being".

* * *

The nature of separate-self is to react because its activities are based on a belief in duality; which means the "center" sees itself as being here and everything else as being out there. This means that it cannot realize clarity, contentment, and joy of the non-duality of "Is-Ness".

* * *

Suffering starts when an individual, or "I", wants to change What-Is-Happening according to its liking or disliking which are layers rooted deep in its so-called sub-conscious mind. Meanwhile, No-Thing-Ness is embracing "ALL" because there are no situations outside of "It-Self" to be improved accordingly. It is "All-There-Is".

* * *

Even the apparent appearance of a separate-self is seemingly is a projection of No-Thing-Ness and at the same time, is not because the appearance is just an illusion. Therefore, everything is and also is not.

* * *

The so-called feeling of lack and fear which are rooted in an individual that is formed out of reactions to beliefs are apparently distorted perceptions of What-Is-Happening, which is seemingly projected on the screen of No-Thing-Ness. This distorted version of What-Is-Happening manifests itself as the feeling of lack and fear that is to be lived by the individual or "me", and so the cycle of Karma goes on, seemingly from one lifetime to another.

* * *

The sensing of What-Is-Happening is "Self-Aware". There is not an individual, or "I", who needs to be aware or be an observer. With this knowing effortlessly comes an understating that there is no one who is being aware as an "observer" and absolute freedom is realized. Next is the dissolution of the individual, and therefore, liberation is realized by no one from

* * *

No-Thing-Ness is "Color-Less" while it is "That", which is the play of "All-Colors".

* * *

So-called thought becomes more and more true by the individual believing in the false concept of being separate from the "Self". While the act of relaxing is taking the isolated thought back to its true nature that is liberated from labeling, programming, or judgment, the thought is the sensing of What-Is-Happening, and as it becomes liberated from its own limitations, it also becomes "Pure-Love-Thought".

* * *

No-Thing-Ness is not withholding anything to satisfy a desire because it is "All-That-Is", fulfilled "As-It-Is".

No-Thing-Ness is not withholding to heal because it is "All-It-Is" as "Ease-Ness" and "All-Well-Ness".

* * *

The individual apparently is fighting against What-Is-Happening in order to get to somewhere else or to find something else. This struggle is what "me" is all about, and its activity to change "What-Is" in order to get to something better seemingly creates more distance and a gap that is never going to be filled with "Truth" by the "me". This process of an individual is like trying to change an image in a mirror, which is pointless.

* * *

What is arising is apparently is being fulfilled by no one. But then again, having a desire and reaction about "What-Is-Arising" is creating a center, and therefore a sense of need to accomplish what each individual has wished for. Consequently, struggling is born out of No-Thing-Ness. Struggling comes in different forms; to get rich, to get well, to be spiritual, to become happy, to become free, to gain enlightenment, to get a partner, to be at peace, and so on.

* * *

The desire of wanting to get better comes from duality.

* * *

The effort that the individual is putting forward to seek the "Truth" is like trying to tie the air into knots or trying to change one's image in the mirror.

* * *

The individual, or "I", as a center, needs time and space to know God in order to give meaning and purpose to its life. To create space, it is forming a "center" (as separate-self) that is here and needs to get there. Also, to create time, it is forming a false sense of separation to find "Self" or "Truth" in the future. The Individual is actually continuing its existence, or its story while it is searching for the "Truth". The actual individual intention is not to find the "Truth", or God, because it knows deep in its psyche that is going to dissolve. Meanwhile, No-Thing-Ness is the sensing of What-Is-Happening in no time and space to no one which is illuminated by the light of Divine in nothing and in everything.

* * *

An Individual, or "me", cannot embrace, accept, forgive, or allow. It is its nature not to surrender. However, No-Thing-Ness is "All-There-Is", open to "All-There-Is" without any resistance to What-Is-Happening. Therefore, forgiving, accepting, embracing, and allowing effortlessly is the true substance of God. A deep understanding of this truth is the dissolution of the individual, who is always putting effort towards achieving something that has never been lost.

* * *

The individual, by making everything so personal, becomes the doer and puts the effort in to get things done, while all along, there is the sensing of What-Is-Happening, which is impersonal toward no one, as no one, through no one.

* * *

The individual, as the separate-self, cannot get rid of thought because it is the thought itself. The "me" is formed by a thought that is believed to be real as an entity. Therefore, "me" cannot distance itself enough to see this truth, and from this point of view, the thought is looking to liberate itself from itself, and so it continues on the path of spirituality for years to come. When thinker and thought disappear into the thinking, what is realized is No-Thing-Ness as "All-There-Is", which is embracing everything.

* * *

After realization, What-Is-Happening is what is happening as Now and ignorance of separate-self, as an individual, is dissolved like it never existed.

* * *

The individual is creating contrast against What-Is-Happening in order to prove it exists through conflicts and wars, while there is no contrast because God is not separated from "It-Self" and in its true nature, is embracing all as unconditional love.

* * *

Getting sick is apparently an effect as the cause in the mind of an individual, while What-Is-Happening is at ease with "All-There-Is".

* * *

The individual is What-Is-Happing knowingly or unknowingly, and arising of a thought which labels, judges, seeks, or searches is the veiling of the "Truth".

* * *

An individual is liberating itself from the illusion of separation when it understands on the deepest level that any seeking or searching for the "Truth" is the veiling of what it is actually looking for. Then and only then, the "Truth" is realized, which causes the dissolution of "me", and return of the individual back to "It-Self" as No-Thing-Ness.

* * *

The action resulting from an individual who believes in separation from its "Source" by way of being ignorant of its true essence, is called sin.

* * *

Whatever an individual has to fight against or to overcome has no effect on the changing of the so-called reality in the outside world because the individual and outside world both do not exist. There is no individual, or "me", who has the power to change an illusion called matter. "All-That-Is" is the movement of No-Thing-Ness that "Is" and "Is-Not" while also being responsive and receptive to its substance.

* * *

The individual does not need to be saved from sin, because there is no "me" or an individual separate from its "Source-of-Being" which is "Fault-Less". The "Source-of-Being" is "Whole-Ness" and is being "All-There-Is" as "Good-Ness" and "Well-Being". Sin is just a thought that is commenting otherwise.

* * *

An individual intention has a deep root in the feeling of lack and fear, and so all its projections are distorted. Trying to change anything in the world of illusion is futile. No amount of effort or struggle can change consequences except the individual realizing its true nature as No-Thing-Ness being "All-Ness".

* * *

Doubt is the reflection of duality and division that is seeded deep in the so-called psyche of the manifested "me" that is reflected on the screen of No-Thing-Ness as uncertainty, doubt, and confusion, while No-Thing-Ness is illuminating duality and non-duality while being "One-With-All".

* * *

Feelings of sadness and anger are just movements of No-Thing-Ness as they are appearing, just to dwindle down to "It-Self" to disappear. When there is no resistance to What-Is-Happening, nothing appears and disappears, and what is realized is the "Absolute-Being".

* * *

An individual that is divided in its nature has the intention of finding a partner so as not to be alone and live in isolation, believing that being lonely is an awful state to live in. Meanwhile, the intention is the movement of What-Is-Happening, whose nature is rejoicing in love and wholeness because it is "All-There-Is", with no separation from the nature of its "Good-Ness".

* * *

No-Thing-Ness is the sensing of What-Is-Happening and appears as diverse forms or different formulations of its original form.

* * *

The individual is playing the role of a successful person, poor person, happy person, anxious person, married person, a divorced person, or a depressed person, and at the source of all these forms is the sensing of What-Is-Happening as the essence of No-Thing-Ness at all times with no relationship to "It-Self".

* * *

No-thing-Ness is not bad or good. It is "Just-Isness" embracing "All-That-Is".

* * *

An individual wants to find meaning for its existence, and search for meaning is its own suffering because What-Is-Happening is not meaningful enough for "me".

82

There is only ignorance of separation to wake up from that would be a remedy to end this suffering.

* * *

A thought needs a thinker, and in the absence of thought and a thinker, the individual dissolves with no trace.

* * *

Apparently, everything, everything, everything is illuminated by the light of No-Thing-Ness and is the sensing of What-Is-Happening on the screen of No-Thing-Ness. Even the so-called reactions coming from an individual with a center is a projection of No-Thing-Ness as No-Thing-Ness by No-Thing-Ness, back unto No-Thing-Ness. Suffering arises when there is an individual with a sense of separation who believes in the duality of being here and the existence of the world out there.

* * *

No-Thing-Ness is the essence that runs through the sensing of What-Is-Happening as thinking, feeling, seeing, hearing, and touching. The essence of No-Thing-Ness is love that does not exclude anything and embraces "All-That-Is". Love is the glue of existence that runs through life, embracing feelings of lack and fear in an individual who believes in separation. The essence of the individual or "worry-center" is love, which cannot separate itself from love. Understanding of this is the recognition of unconditional love.

* * *

There are no limitations or conditioning. These are all movements of God. The reaction which arises from ignorance, on the other hand, is an act that creates a sense of separation, and as its result, "worry-me" is born and, therefore, too pain and suffering.

* * *

Inquiry into "who am I?" is a good start on this journey but expecting an individual to find an answer is the very obstacle that is veiling the "Truth". When there is no expectation of wanting to find the "Truth" or expectation of something to happen, "me" is dissolved, and so too are all the thoughts around the assumption of God being out there and an individual being here. What is remaining is No-Thing-Ness as the sensing of being aware of sensing as "Self-Being-Aware".

* * *

Ignorance of being separate from the "Source" creates the illusion of the world and its suffering. The world is apparently a projection of the What-Is-Happening on the screen of No-Thing-Ness. Being an individual with a center which creates a relationship and, therefore, reaction with the world, is creating suffering. When the "me" or "worry-center" disappears, so does the relationship and the world as "I" knows it. All that remains and is realized is No-Thing-Ness as the essence of all is well and unconditional love.

* * *

No ignorance, no reaction, no separation, no thought, no "I", no reaction, no world, and no suffering from.

* * *

No-Thing-Ness is impersonal. By trying to have a personal relationship colored by judgments and reactions, the "I" makes this impersonal, blissful relationship the cause of its suffering.

84

* * *

When "worry-center" is dissolved, so too are distorted thoughts and emotions which are colored by the feelings of lack and fear. What is realized is No-Thing-Ness being "All-There-Is" as the sensing of What-Is-Happening, which is forming itself as love and harmonious thoughts and feelings which remain impersonal in the field of unconditional love.

* * *

A thought is arising, and a reaction to that thought creates a thinker, which gives an appearance of an "I" who is going to experience the cause and effect of this phenomenon as action and reaction. As long as "I" believes in being separate from its "Source", its story will continue in the field of "Time-Less" and "Space-Less".

* * *

An individual who is the doer dissolves in love, and all that remains is No-Thing-Ness as "All-There-Is" as a doer, what is done, and by what the doer is doing.

An individual who sees, dissolves in love, and all that remains is No-Thing-Ness as "All-There-Is" as a seer, the seen, and seeing.

An individual who perceives is dissolved in love, and all that remains is No-Thing-Ness as "All-There-Is" as a perceiver, perceived, and perceiving.

An individual who is perceived to be a separate-self dissolves in love, and all that remains is No-Thing-Ness as "All-There-Is" as the lover, beloved, and loving.

* * *

When there is no doer, what remains is What-Is-Happening in its "Full-Ness", "Fresh-Ness", and "New-

Ness". It is "Is-Ness" as the "Full-Essence-of-God," and as unconditional love. Total sincere surrendering to the so-called moment and ultimate allowing of No-Thing-Ness to express "It-Self" as "It-Self", by "It-self", through "It-Self", projects universal and unconditional happiness and blessings for no one to experience as the "Whole-Ness".

* * *

Being aware as an observer, in order to find the "Truth" is actually veiling the "Truth".

* * *

Apparently, every individual mind and body has its own unique pattern and layers of conditioning which are being illuminated by the light of No-Thing-Ness as "Uni-Verse" (the metrical rhythm of the song), expressing "It-Self" as love, compassion, kindness, harmony, peace, and vitality. These expressions that are being illuminated by the light of No-Thing-Ness metaphorically like the ocean which forms as a drop of water, wave, and current in the uncompromising ocean. All these changeable forms apparently come into existence from the point of view of No-Thing-Ness, which is "Un-Moveable", "Un-Changeable", and "Un-Avoidable" as being "All-There-Is".

* * *

As the sunlight shines through water drops to make a rainbow, so does No-Thing-Ness illuminate various forms to reflect on the screen of God's Mind the "Uni-Verse" as "One-Song" in harmony.

* * *

An individual or "me" is afraid of dying. Perhaps that is why surrendering completely to God's will is so difficult as it is the end of the drama of the individual and its disappearance back to No-Thing-Ness.

* * *

There is no desire as there is no individual to desire. What-Is-Happening as desire is fulfilled without any effort on the part of an individual or "I".

* * *

There is no individual who is seeing with an eye or tasting with a tongue. Seeing spontaneously is as What-Is-Happening, followed by a thought, colored by a belief which labels the whole process by way of an "I", who is seeing. There is no eye that sees, no nose that smells, and no ear that hears. Seeing, hearing, touching, smelling, tasting are all spontaneously happening.

* * *

Seeing is a phenomenon as What-is-Happening and not direct functionality of an eye that sees.

Hearing is a phenomenon as What-Is-Happening and not direct functionality of an ear that hears.

Tasting is a phenomenon as What-Is-Happening and not direct functionality of a tongue that tastes.

Smelling is a phenomenon as What-Is-Happening and not direct functionality of a nose that smells.

Touching is a phenomenon as What-is-Happening and not direct functionality of skin that touches.

* * *

There is no individual that is experiencing No-Thing-Ness as an extraordinary experience. No-Thing-Ness is the sensing of What-Is-Happening as both ordinary and extraordinary and is happening for no one. Abiding in the sensing, which is being aware of sensing (being self-aware) is an ultimate practice, which means "total-rest" or "total-surrender" by no one and for no one.

* * *

When the individual is liberating "It-Self" from not being this and not being that, rather the "Essence-of-Love", it merges into No-Thing-Ness and realizes "It-Self" as the "Absolute-Being".

* * *

There is no individual, or "I", who is taking action to make things happen. When effort is needed, "Effort-Less" appears.

* * *

When healing apparently is needed, well-being appears as What-Is-Happening until it is not, all spontaneously.

When hearing apparently is needed, the sound appears as What-Is-Happening until it is not, all spontaneously.

When seeing apparently is needed, sight appears as What-Is-Happening until it is not, all spontaneously.

When touching apparently is needed, a touch appears as What-Is-Happening until it is not, all spontaneously.

When tasting apparently is needed, taste appears as What-Is-Happening until it is not, all spontaneously.

When smelling apparently is needed, smell appears as What-Is-Happening until it is not, all spontaneously.

When thinking apparently is needed, thought appears as What-Is-Happening until it is not, all spontaneously.

When being/feeling apparently is needed, bodily-sensation appears as What-Is-Happening until it is not, all spontaneously.

* * *

An individual, whose existence is based on cause and effect apparently repeats itself over and over again (as long as there is a reaction which is arising from ignorance) in a cycle of recurrence called Karma. The only time the "I", or individual, is out of the whirlpool (torment) or the vicious cycle of cause and effect is when "worry-center" is liberated by realizing No-Thing-Ness as "Choice-Less", "Change-Less", and "Ease-Ness". With this understating, the story or drama of the center called "me" ends.

* * *

Apparently, after birth, No-Thing-Ness identifies "It-Self" with two sense perceptions of the mind and body to manifest the concept of an individual and with five sense perceptions to perceive the world by that individual. Identification entirely with the world, mind, and body gives a sense of a "center" being as a mind and body and perception of the world out-there. The sense of separation stays with an individual throughout its lifetime as being a separate entity until it is not.

* * *

There is no effort on the part of an individual to take any action because the individual does not exist. A thought arises, so then a deed is taken to fulfill it without any effort or delay, which the individual calls a miracle. After a desire is fulfilled, a thought arises to take ownership for making it happen as a miracle worker. *Without a doer, there is neither thought, nor thinker, nor thinking.*

* * *

Observer, observed, and observation are all different forms of No-Thing-Ness, but labeling them gives the impression that they are all being different entities; meanwhile, everything appears and disappears in No-Thing-Ness.

* * *

It is not even about What-Is-Happening but instead is about sensing of What-Is-Happening as a feeling. As thought reacts to an impersonal emotion, it creates the feeling of frustration or confusion, meanwhile the sensing by means of unconditional love holds the feeling of frustration and confusion in clarity and feeing of fear in love and compassion.

* * *

An individual hears about being aware and gets this wrong impression on the intellectual level that there is an "I" who is aware. In the sensing, there is no impression as an individual who is sensing but sensing of What-Is-Happening is just happening, which comes from a deep level of existence.

* * *

There is nothing wrong with the apparent world, but the individual who is illusory, believes it to be otherwise. As a matter of fact, the distortion comes from the false self, which apparently is the cause of the confusion and is the confusion itself.

* * *

There is a doer or an individual who is seeking enlightenment, but the sensing of devotion (longing for reality), sensing of liberation (yearning for freedom), and sensing of love for the Absolute (desiring for the beloved) is the way back to the realization of No-Thing-Ness.

* * *

There is no individual with a center as a subject and a world out there as an object, because "me", or the "center", is a false concept. Identification with a body, mind, and the world creates a sense of separation and judgment, and labeling creates more separation (distorting or limiting of What-Is-Happening as caused by reaction). Therefore, there is only the sensing of What-Is-Happening, the source of all creation, that is from within, which manifests the concepts of the world, mind, and body. There is no mind, a body, or the world. When the sensing is intended towards the outside from the point view of What-Is-Happening, the concept of world, mind, and body are created, and when the sensing is aimed within from the point view of almost no movement or the subtlest movement of What-Is-Happening, then No-Thing-Ness is realized as God. If it recognized, first is the realization of unconditional love and peace as purest form and later on a deeper level as No-Thing-Ness, the "Absolute-Being".

* * *

The way to become a pure vibration is to know that deeply:

Judgment is the cause of suffering.

Jealousy is the cause of suffering.

Desire is the cause of suffering.

Attachment is the cause of suffering.

Labeling is the cause of suffering.

Identification is the cause of suffering.

The feelings of fear and lack are the cause of suffering.

* * *

After the realization, the memory of an individual disappears like a patient who is put to sleep for surgery and does not remember anything about the operation. So too, is the individual who has lived a life with all its drama and stories.

* * *

Sensing the essence of love does not mean that there is an individual who loves others; instead, it just means that loving is being aware of loving, or better said, "All-Is-Love". Love is aware of love as "Love-Is".

* * *

All is happening as the sensing of What-Is-Happening without any doer until a thought arises with a concept or a belief that "I am not liberated" and that notion simply creates a "center" and the world of duality that "I" has to live and suffer from. It is just a thought that is the self itself that separates the "I" from its true nature by the power of Maya.

* * *

There is order and harmony in the movement of No-Thing-Ness as it is spontaneously arising and fading away. These movements or impulses are labeled by the individual as law. The so-called impersonal thoughts and desires are arising and being fulfilled and disappear. All are happening in the so-called field of "Omnipresent", "Omnipotent", and "Omniscient".

* * *

Sensing is the language of the inner world and comes deeply from the substance of creation. When sensing, the creator is creating its own creation as tasting, seeing, touching, hearing, smelling, thinking, and feeling, while at the same time, sensing is being aware of sensing as No-Thing-Ness that is "All-There-Is".

* * *

With eyes open, the sensing of What-Is-Happening and therefore projection and appearance of the mind, body, and the world, and as the eye closes, the inner world of No-Thing-Ness is sensed and consequently, the disappearance of mind, body, and the world.

* * *

CHAPTER 4

Liberation from the Illusionary World

L iberation is just the free movement of What-Is-Happening that no longer is being limited or overshadowed by the "center" or "me". The "center" or "me" is perceiving being a "center" here and assuming a world out there.

* * *

Even after what it can be called waking up, the "One-Ness" plays the game of hide and seek. The "me" or individual, as a separate-self, might arise and identify itself with "me", but the momentum is gone. All that remains is thought or feeling arising, and there is no story or drama for the "worry-center" to sustain its apparent separation.

* * *

A so-called thought might be arising, or a feeling, which is the same as though with more force or charge, but because the seeker or individual is gone, the force cannot sustain itself as the thought or feeling and therefore goes back as a neutral movement to its original state of "Non-Existence".

* * *

We have stopped "Being" for the sake of doing. Having an agenda and purpose, even at its highest virtue, is limiting the freedom that the individual is craving so desperately. In the meantime, liberation or freedom is What-Is-Happening by no one and to no one.

* * *

What is happening all around is a miracle. No-Thing-Ness and its essence have been named and described in many ways:

It is compassionate because it embraces everything.

It is love because its existence is not in the past nor in the future to be affected by the feelings of fear, lack, and worry.

It is peace because there is nothing in "It-Self" to deny "It-Self".

It heals because its essence is ease, and it does not know about dis-ease.

It is abundance because there is no limitation or lack when it comes to its existence as it embraces all and complete.

It is "Time-Less" because it is here, there, nowhere, and everywhere.

It matters one moment and does not the next because it is "Substance-Less".

It is "End-Less" because it cannot be ceased or terminated.

It is the very existence of What-Is-Happening because it is the absolute "Being-Ness".

It is "Time-Less" because it has no start and no end.

It is "Infinite" and at the same time, a "Limited" or a "finite" version of "It-Self".

It is a joy because not even for a moment separated from its nature, which is "In-Joy".

It is "All-There-Is" because there is nothing outside "It-Self" to deny itself as it is "Infinite".

It is harmless because there is nothing outside of it to harm or to be harmed as it is "All-There-Is".

It is fulfilled because it is not in search of fulfillment as it is "Self-Actualized" and "Self-Fulfilled".

It is a sense of well-being because it is not separate from its essence as "All-Is-Well".

It cannot be found because it is "Never-Lost".

It cannot be understood because it is "Empty-Ness".

It cannot be denied because it is "All-There-Is".

* * *

There could be an analytical answer to all the questions of the world to satisfy the mind, but there is always another issue in need of a solution. The basis for these inquiries arises from the sense of separation, and this gap of separation will never be filled by the mind or its questions and answers until it realizes its true nature. Mind, body, birth, and death are What-Is-Happening. There is no complication or obstacle that needs to be looked at or a puzzle to be solved. It is What-Is-Happing for no-body and to no one.

* * *

True Liberation is liberation from seeking.

* * *

No-Thing-Ness in its movement is as free as What-Is-Happening. At one moment, it is seemingly chattering, another moment it is sleeping, and the next moment is drinking with no meaning or purpose. The individual or "worry-center" is framing or naming the processes to control it and, therefore, to make itself feel secure, which is the very cause of insecurity.

* * *

No-thing-Ness is called "Not-Two", which is so we don't say it is "One". If we say it is "One", then it must have an element outside of the "One" to know itself, and consequently, it must have a relationship between the knower and known or a "center" here and there and therefore, the concept of duality is formed. "All-There-Is" is No-Thing-Ness.

* * *

Our assumption of what liberation or freedom must look like is what is keeping the "Truth" hidden from us.

* * *

The "Known", which is the individual cannot know the "Un-Known".

* * *

The individual is making What-Is-Happening, which is impersonal, personal by naming it. This process of labeling hides the sensing of "What-Is", which is No-Thing-Ness from "me" and therefore the game of lost and found is born, which gives the "I" purpose and goal to continue.

* * *

"Self" is nothing as No-Thing-Ness, and "Self" is everything as the sensing of What-Is-Happening; the "Alive-Ness" of "All-There-Is".

* * *

When the so-called realization happens, the body or mind does not wake up, but the "Alive-Ness" becomes self-aware, which is always "Self-Aware" but is hidden under the assumption of a belief that someone is waking up. "Truth" is so simple and obvious, and yet it is distorted by the seeker, and therefore, it is hidden.

* * *

The No-Thing-Ness is seemingly arising and disappearing by activities of "It-Self".

* * *

The thought is seemingly arising. It is What-Is-Happening in its purest form, apparently manifesting as thinking.

Sight is seemingly arising. It is What-Is-Happening in its purest form, apparently manifesting as seeing.

The bodily-sensation is seemingly arising. It is What-Is-Happening in its purest form, apparently manifesting as the being.

The aroma is seemingly arising. It is What-Is-Happening in its purest form, apparently manifesting as smelling.

Emotion is seemingly arising. It is What-Is-Happening in its purest form, apparently manifesting as feeling.

No-Thing-Ness is the sensing of What-Is-Happening in its purest form, apparently as compassion, well-being, love, peace, happiness, and joy as "It-Self", by "It-Self", to "It-Self" and back unto "It-Self".

* * *

No-Thing-Ness is "All-There-Is". It is being aware of being "Self-Aware", so it does not need anything outside of itself to know itself.

* * *

With being self-aware comes no reaction and the realization of "Not-Two" for no one.

* * *

Liberation is what is realized by no one. The so-called process to surrender, to let go, trust, and abide by the power of grace, which is happening to nobody.

* * *

Surrendering is apparently an attempt to find "Truth" by the power of grace, which is what is happening to no one.

* * *

There is no "I", "me", or "mine" that is separate from the totality of "All-There-Is". There is no ego standing alone as an isolated part that has been left by itself to control, struggle and put the effort forth to survive. Searching for the pursuit of happiness is going to veil the "Truth", which is always liberated from the seeker. While seeking is happening, its true nature, which is well-being and peace is happening to no one.

* * *

A liberated, free movement of a vibration seemingly becomes thought, then sensation and perception. Any reaction to any so-called state of mind makes this apparent natural process personal. Therefore, it becomes an experience that must be experienced by an individual or by "I".

* * *

This message appears as the last message, which stops the earnest seeker who is running out of options to become enlightened. The message is for those who finally understand and realize the true nature of "I" as a false sense of separation with no existence of its own. This is a state that God is realized because "I" is not. Consequently, God realizes itself as God.

* * *

Another meaning for liberation is embracing "All-That-Is", which is "Love" that embraces good and bad, wrong and right, dark and light, mortality and immortality, bondage and freedom, ease and disease, lack and abundance, and hate and kindness.

* * *

Waking up and seeing that everything "As-It-Is" is normal and ordinary while creating a world of illusion and living in it like it is real is actually abnormal.

* * *

Dissolution of separate-self is the appearance of "One-Ness" that was hidden in the most obvious way all along.

* * *

No-Thing-Ness is "All-There-Is". That is why it is liberated and is "Self-Aware".

* * *

The disease, frustration, suffering, struggling, and effort all are so-called pointers that are referring to what is already liberated and free as being more productive, happier, healthier, and more fulfilled as being "What-Is".

* * *

An attempt to fixing "That", which is not broken is futile.

Pointing to "What-Is-Pointless", which is useless.

Wanting to make sense of something "Substance-Less" is meaningless.

Hoping to label or frame What-Is-Happening in order to make sense of it is hopeless.

* * *

Releasing a desire to understand What-Is-Happening is like a journey taken to the deepest part of the so-called individual to find nothing and everything as No-Thing-Ness.

* * *

Utterly and desperately seeking to find "Truth" that is going on is also the game of hide-and-seek for no one.

* * *

The true meaning of liberation is that there is no longer anyone who is searching or seeking to fix it, make it better, make it more meaningful, or become prosperous and happier. There is nothing or no one outside of "Liberated-Self" to judge, and eventually, this realization dissolves the "worry-center".

* * *

No-Thing-Ness is the sensing of What-Is-Happening with no story but apparently with its movements of arising and fading away, illuminating and forming as an individual who has a story to tell and live separate from its "Source".

* * *

After the so-called shadow of separate-self falls away, what remains is the sensing of What-Is-Happening. The sensing of being aware of being "Self-Aware" is thusly liberated and being illuminated as the light of No-Thing-Ness.

* * *

Being in a so-called state of no desire, no hope, no striving, and no will seem like a state of demise, which in a way is as much as the death of an individual or "me" as it is when "I" wakes up from the dream of separation. "I" is liberated from seeking, and all that remains is "Liberated-Self" as the "One".

* * *

An individual or "worry-center" cannot find the so-called state of freedom while always bounded by its contradiction as contraction.

* * *

There is no God in the future that can be found. A future God is the projection of the separate-self. It is just a dream and story in the imagination of an individual. "Worry-center" or better said, the seeker, always puts God in the distance from itself for seeking so it may continue to find more purification, more reading, more understating, and more spiritual practice in any shape and form. Always this appears as a feeling of not-quite-there-yet. It is a feeling that there is a God that is around the corner. More theories, philosophy, and views about what

God should be, place the God, the one and the only that is so close and attainable, in the distance.

* * *

The individual seeking of God creates the appearance of separation, and with it comes the search for the pursuit of happiness as a story to be lived, but in vain.

* * *

When full alignment happens, there is no longer cause and effect, no longer ease or disease, no longer right or wrong, rather liberation and freedom that is happening to no one. It is a realization that "I" or individual sense of separation never existed.

* * *

With realization, the belief in a solid body and concept of here and there drops, and all remain is "Illuminated-Body" as the temple of God.

* * *

When "I", individual, or separate-self falls away, the so-called contradiction falls away, and all that remains is the realization that What-Is-Happening is in its purest form as No-Thing-Ness.

* * *

Liberation is not happening because separate-self surrenders itself to get "It" or find "It". The seeker who is seeking is restricted by its nature and cannot find the "Un-Limited" and the "Empty-Ness". Meanwhile, the seeker, seeking, and what is sought are liberated as the sensing of What-Is-Happening.

* * *

Liberation is the freedom from the activity of separate-self. Its movement is impersonal in a relationship with the separate-self. Freedom is free from being personal or becoming entangled by having a relationship with an entity who has a dramatic story of being a victim.

* * *

The so-called grace is the light of the No-Thing-Ness that is shining and brings clarity to the darkness of the ignorance of separate-self. While all of these metaphors are being said, What-Is-Happening is happening as the light, illuminated by No-Thing-Ness. All there is, is "This", embracing All and holding on to nothing, as its essence is love, but yet it is not what is labeled as love.

* * *

Surrendering is the sensing of What-Is-Happening as liberation rather than an activity of an individual who wants to liberate itself to have more control and power for a better, happier life. No-Thing-Ness is the "Is-Ness" with no motivation and no willpower outside of its existence, and therefore, no cause for surrendering.

* * *

Thought, therefore, thinking, is a desire of an individual or "me" to find the missing God. Liberation is the realization of the truth that nothing is lost, and What-Is-Happening is "All-There-Is" without a "worry-center" and its story of absent God.

* * *

The layers of so-called beliefs, names, titles, behaviors, and habits are what is limiting the freedom of what is already the "Liberated-One".

* * *

Liking and disliking of thoughts create distortion, and therefore, an illusion. Without the distortion, no illusion remains, and "Liberated-Reality" is shining all the time.

* * *

There is no "me," no "I", no "mine", and therefore no reaction, no distortion, and no illusion. Liberation is shining "As-It-Is" through no one and to no one.

* * *

No-Thing-Ness shines in the absence of an individual or a "worry-center". What else can be more liberating than knowing this truth?

* * *

Another name for No-Thing-Ness in religious terms is God, which is happening in the so-called now, but it does not need time to realize "It-Self". It is "Self-Realized" by no one. The phrase "hiding and finding" used by the seeker is What-Is-Happening when it is liberated and free as "That".

* * *

What-Is-Happening is appearing as different forms like seeking, hearing, thinking, and feeling. Similar to the different kinds of waves and inner currents; they are all part of the ocean, and not separate from the totality of the ocean even for a moment.

* * *

Taking the label off of hate, all which remains is liberated from limitation as love.

Taking the label off of fear, all which remains is liberated from limitation as love.

Taking the label off of lack, all which remains is liberated from limitation as love.

* * *

The individual or "worry-center", without any agenda is "That", which embraces and accomplishes All without claiming any victory. Apparently, it is its nature as the "All-Knowing" to meet effortlessly the need of every moment as it arises.

* * *

Where there is no "me" or a "worry-center", apparently a feeling of anger arises, and it is liberated as the sensing of What-Is-Happening as compassion.

Where there is no "me" or a "worry-center", apparently a feeling of fear arises and is liberated as the sensing of What-Is-Happening as courage.

Where there is no "me" or a "worry-center", apparently a feeling of lack arises, liberated as the sensing of What-Is-Happening as abundance.

* * *

This message is liberating because "That", which is No-Thing-Ness, is "All-There-Is", as "Every-Thing" and "No-Thing" for no one. There is nothing that is going to be found, learned, discovered, realized, revealed, or understood, outside of "That". An observer as an entity has to go outside of itself to observe "That", but the observer, observed and observing is "That" too.

* * *

Apparently knowing that What-Is-Happening is meaningless or hopeless is liberating because the truth of it is taking away the urge of being hopeful, eager, ambitious, and motivated, all of which are the driving force of an individual or "worry-center", and puts the "I" out of existence. At the same time, there is no longer a process of thinking that is comparing What-Is-Happening to the memory of what has happened to make a continuous story for the doer to tell. "Empty-Ness" stands alone, liberated, and unconditionally fulfilled in real-time as No-Thing-Ness as the "Illuminated-Self" with no past and future. It is happening as the sensing of What-Is-Happening in Now, as Now, back unto Now.

* * *

Liberation is the realization that there is no doer as "I", and that there is not something that is done but only What-Is-Happening by the form of doing by no one.

Liberation is the realization that there is no seer as "I", and that there is not something that is seen but only What-Is-Happening by the form of seeing by no one.

Liberation is the realization that there is no thinker as "I", and that there is not something that is thought but only What-Is-Happening by the form of thinking by no one.

Liberation is the realization that there is no being as "I", and that there is not something that is felt but only What-Is-Happening by the form of the feeling by no one.

Liberation is the realization that there is no listener as "I", and that there is not something that is listened to but only What-Is-Happening by the form of listening by no one.

Liberation is the realization that there is no observer as "I", and that there is not something that is observed but only What-Is-Happening by the form of the act of observing by no one.

Liberation is the realization that there is no healer as "I", and that there is not something that needs to be healed but only What-Is-Happening by the form of the act of healing by no one.

* * *

Apparently, thought is arising, and the response is seemingly the natural, ordinary, and harmonious movement of No-Thing-Ness to fulfill the need around that so-called thought, with no story attached. For example, there is a thought arising with an expression of going for a walk, and spontaneous action comes in the form of getting ready to go out for a walk with no story attached around the action. In the case of "me" or an individual, the thought is arising, and there is a response to fulfill the need just as before, but apparently, a reaction takes place instead of a response. The reaction is colored and limited by stories like "I am too tired to go for a walk," or "it is cold or hot," or "my back is hurting," and therefore a feeling of stress is created by not taking the responsive action. Stress is amplified by the consequence of non-action (or action) and more reaction and drama surrounding it. The layers and layers of reactions as conditioning cover responses that could have been so natural without the story of "I" or individual, which continues to exist for some time. Liberation is the fulfillment of an apparent need by the free movement and not by the reaction that has been colored by a limitation of an illusion called "I", which is a projection of ignorance, that distorts the "Truth".

* * *

Apparently, surrendering of the so-called mind from seeking to be the liberated-one is liberation.

Apparently, surrendering of this so-called body from seeking to be the illuminated-one is liberation.

Apparently, surrendering of this so-called heart from seeking to be the loving-one is liberation.

* * *

Every moment is self-aware and seemingly contains that which in its nature is peace, love, harmony, well-being, and happiness, all of which are unfolding most ordinarily as the "Extra-Ordinary" and always gracefully, harmoniously, and effortlessly.

* * *

No-Thing-Ness is unconditioned and not divided against itself, free of ignorance of separation, and therefore, with no sense of separate-self. It is the "Limit-Less" free being limited as "me". There is no beginning to its existence, and there is no end because it is "All-There-Is" as "Is-Ness". It is "Self-Aware" and liberated to "It-Self", by "It-Self", in "It-Self", as "It-Self".

* * *

Liberation, awakening, enlightenment, self-realization, salvation, illumination, and nirvana are words to describe the dissolution of ignorance and realization of No-Thing-Ness as "Death-Less", "Time-Less", "Empty-Ness", and "Space-Less".

* * *

There is no effort that is going to tear down the veil because there is no one or any individual to do that. The effortless movement of sensing as What-Is-Happening sees through the veil, and with a deep understanding and a sense of remembering comes the realization that there is no individual, nor any separation. Apparently, What-Is-

Happening is appearing as the sense of an individual who is seeking or struggling until it is not.

* * *

So-called thought becomes more and more hardened and complicated by the conditioning of a sense of separation, which is caused by ignorance. Apparently, lessening or relaxing is taking thought back to its true nature of being as What-Is-Happening, liberated, and free from its deep programming of being a separate entity who has a choice to think.

* * *

There is seemingly sensitivity and understating to What-Is-Happening, to the point that any subtle arising is being seen by the light of No-Thing-Ness, which is called clarity. The individual is not going to realize this because its nature is based on ambiguity, which is also a lack of transparency. Liberation is the clarity and knowingness of What-Is-Happening, as "All-Knowing" and "Not-Knowing".

* * *

To realize the "Is-Ness" of this moment free from any noise is liberation.

* * *

Suffering is a reaction to the distorted form of What-Is-Happening, and liberation is an attunement to the grace of What-Is-Happening.

* * *

Sensing of What-Is-Happening is not a state that an individual can get in and out of. It is No-Thing-Ness as the sensing of What-Is-Happening, harmonious without any distortion or interruption. Being in-tune with itself with no interruption allows for peace that has passed all understanding and so too for liberation from a sense of separation.

* * *

Liberation is an understanding that no effort is needed to be put forth, and that there is a spontaneous response to the fulfillment of a deed in every moment.

Liberation is an understating that everything out there is the reflection of "What-Is".

Liberation is freedom from believing that there is an individual with all its stories and drama.

* * *

Liberation is the sensing of "All-Is-Well".
Liberation is the sensing of "All-Is-At-Ease".
Liberation is the sensing of "All-Is-One".
Liberation is the sensing of "All-There-Is".
Liberation is the sensing of "All-Is-In-Joy".
Liberation is the sensing of "All-Is-Peace".
Liberation is the sensing of "All-Is-Free".
Liberation is the sensing of "All-Is-Flawless".
Liberation is the sensing of "All-Is-Good".
Liberation is the sensing of "All-Is-In-Harmony".
Liberation is the sensing of "All-Is-Love".
Liberation is the sensing of "All-Is-Light".
Liberation is the sensing of "All-Is-God".

* * *

As soon as the argument of being a separate-self is over, freedom and liberation are restored, and all that remains is the sensing of What-Is-Happening as "All-There-Is" without a second. Liberation is the realization of "That".

* * *

There is no searching or seeking liberation except dropping all the arguments that the individual or "me" is not "That". Apparently, becoming in-tune with peace and joy is the sensing of What-Is-Happing in the most natural way that knows no resistance or any effort on the so-called path of enlightenment.

* * *

There is nothing to know because there is nothing out there except the No-Thing-Ness as What-Is-Happening. This is liberation from seeking. Wanting to gain more knowledge on the intellectual level is actually veiling the very "Truth" that the individual is searching for.

* * *

Apparently, there is only one desire; the universal desire to be liberated from the sense of separation, which is based on ignorance in order to shine by "It-Self" as the rays of light.

* * *

The individual is liberating itself from the illusion of separation when it realizes that any seeking or searching for the "Truth" is covering what it is looking for. Then, and only then is the realized "I" and with it the dissolution of "me" and the return of the individual back to itself as No-Thing-Ness, that is "All-Ness".

* * *

The essence of No-Thing-Ness is the light that shines over the so-called separated part of itself as "me" that is conditioned by the layers of fear and lack. The light of Divine shines over the shadow of ignorance of the individual in order for the "worry-center" to come out of the darkness of being a separate-self and realize itself as being part of the "Whole-Ness". Apparently, the process is called enlightenment, healing, and liberation.

* * *

In "One-Ness" is "All-Ness", which at its core is liberated and free.

* * *

Because No-Thing-Ness is already the love, so the appearance of "I" is the lover and beloved.

Because No-Thing-Ness is already free, so the appearance of "I" is the liberated one.

Because No-Thing-Ness is already at peace, so the appearance of "I" is peaceful.

Because No-Thing-Ness is already feeling joy, so the appearance of "I" is joyful.

Because No-Thing-Ness is already blissed, so the appearance of "I" is blissful.

* * *

No-Thing-Ness is illuminated, fulfilled "As-Is", and liberated without a second.

No-Thing-Ness is illuminated, peaceful "As-Is", and free without a second.

* * *

Seemingly realization of "One-Ness" and "All-Ness" appearing as the sensing of What-Is-Happening and, therefore, dissolution of "me" or the individual back into No-Thing-Ness is freedom from the world of duality. Apparently, the state of duality is the cause for the appearance of the world, and the state of non-duality is the cause for the disappearance of the world back to "Cause-Less".

* * *

The light of No-Thing-Ness shines to dispel the shadows of lack, fear, and dis-ease like the ray of sunshine.

* * *

That which is changing cannot know the "Change-Less".

That which is moving cannot know the "Immovable".

That which is divided cannot know the "Whole-Ness".

That which is mortal cannot know the "Immortal".

That which is bounded cannot know the "Bound-Less".

That which is finite cannot know the "Infinite".

That which is known cannot know the "Un-known".

That which is limited cannot know the "Limit-Less".

That which is bounded by time cannot know the "Time-Less".

That which is full cannot know the "Empty-Ness".

* * *

Liberation (embracing What-Is-Happening) dissolves the illusion of a separate-self. It is an understanding that it is not about the individual who needs to get rid of ego who wants to become enlightened, but it is about waking up from a dream of an illusionary, false-self who is seeking enlightenment.

* * *

The individual is on the path when it is going back on a journey from the material world, to the perceiving world, and from the perceiving world to the sensing of What-Is-Happening, and to the sensing, which is being aware of the sensing as being "Self-Aware", back to No-Thing-Ness, to realize Divine. This is a process called neti neti, literally means neither this nor that. And in the next breath, going back to embrace and to claim back, everything as the essence of the Divine.

* * *

There is no desire that is separate from What-Is-Happening. Within What-Is-Happening arises a desire and it is met with the fulfilling of it, liberated from any efforting or struggling.

* * *

Liberation is a realization that suffering is an illusion because there is no individual who is suffering.

Liberation is a realization that seeking is an illusion because there is nothing outside of the "Self" to seek for.

Liberation is a realization that struggling is an illusion because there is nothing to strive for.

* * *

All the questions are presented by the individual or "worry-center" are because the "I" is sensing separation. Nothing can heal this gap because separation from No-Thing-Ness is ignorance of the "Truth". Deep understanding of this truth results in the liberation and dissolution of "I" and realization of the essence of No-Thing-Ness as love and compassion by no one and for no one.

* * *

The so-called distortion that is formed by a belief in the feeling of lack and fear as the darkness of ignorance has no existence in the presence of "Light-of-Love".

* * *

There is no limitation or conditioning. They are all the movements of God. There is only the reaction out of ignorance that creates a sense of separation, and therefore, "worry-center" is born out of thin air.

* * *

Being aware as an observer who wants to get enlightened is the veiling of the "Truth".

* * *

Every mind and body has its own unique pattern and layers of conditioning. Seemingly, when it is being illuminated by the light of No-Thing-Ness, like the musical beat of the song, is expressing "It-Self" as intense energy of light as a different spectrum of love as a "Being". These vibrations are the harmonic rhythm of life and the vitality that comes from the "Source".

* * *

When the individual is liberated by its own deliverance, it becomes like the currents, waves, and a drop of water; free to be "What-Is", dancing to the rhythm of every moment as what the expression of Divine wants it to be. All these changeable forms apparently come to existence from the point of view of No-Thing-Ness, which is "Un-Moveable", "Un-Changeable", and "Un-Avoidable", because it is "All-There-Is" and liberated from "It-Self" in and with its own emptiness.

* * *

Any attempt to become free is a veil over the very freedom and liberation that "worry-center" is seeking.

* * *

The world is being seen through the same eyes of the "Liberated-One" as an individual. The only difference is that the "Liberated-One" knows the world as "It-Self" while the "worry-center" does not and is living in chaos as the separate-one.

CHAPTER 5

Mind, Body, and the World

The so-called body is the resonance and reflection of the sensing of What-Is-Happening. An individual who is making things happen, such as listing to music or seeing a movie, is pure expression and projection of What-Is-Happening as a body for nobody.

* * *

The so-called body is resonating with the vibration of What-Is-Happening, causing hearing, seeing, tasting, and touching to happen. With deep understanding and clarity comes the realization that there is no physical object but only the illusion of an object being there, just like an image in the mirror. The world is only the reflection and projection of What-Is-Happening. This apparently creates an illusion of a world and perception of an individual which is separate from "It Self".

* * *

There is not actually a solid body with an "I" inside of it. The "I" as a doer has always been trying to get, to do, to find, and even to "Be". The "I" cannot "Be" because its nature is not based on being but is instead based on seeking. To Summarize:

Apparently, the body is effortlessly hearing with an instrument called an ear.

Apparently, the body is effortlessly seeing with an instrument called an eye.

Apparently, the body is effortlessly smelling with an instrument called a nose.

Apparently, the body is effortlessly being with an instrument called the body.

Apparently, the body is effortlessly thinking with an instrument called a mind.

* * *

There is a so-called thought due to a desire that is arising, and spontaneously, there is a response to fulfill its need with actions. For example, there is a sense of thirst that is arising and spontaneously is followed by an activity, such as drinking a glass of water. There is no "I", "me", or an individual with a story but rather simple, spontaneous arising of actions as "Is-Ness". In this state of "Just-Isness", life seems to become effortless and very simple.

* * *

There is no cause and effect. Cause and effect happen when there are actions and reactions based on an individual with memory and therefore a story. When the response comes spontaneously with no story surrounding it, that response is What-Is-Happening and displays no apparent cause and effect. But the "worry-center" thrives on the drama. The fundamental nature of drama is to keep creating a story of not-this and not-that, which continues the search for happiness.

* * *

Apparently, if there is a pain in the body, the body is intelligent enough to take care of its own needs. If there is a headache, the body will take care of its need by taking spontaneous action or no action to heal itself. More of life is as simple as that. What actually is happening is the internal judgment around the chronic symptom that is creating a false action plan, which in turn is causing more pain and therefore sustaining suffering.

* * *

Any resistance to natural body sensations creates pain, and reaction to the pain creates more suffering.

* * *

The stories that the individual is telling are based on lack and fear, both of which stem from a sense of separation. They are stories to keep the individual, or "me" safe, protecting the self from its own dissolution, which means the death of the individual.

* * *

There is a sense of localization or center, that seems to be in the body because the body believes itself to be real and solid. This belief manifests itself as a doer having choices. There is also a belief that there is an "I", or an individual who is a creator and creates reality by the power of the mind. This belief manifests itself as an "I" who lives in the world. Questioning the false belief of being a center as an "I" who has the power to choose or to create reality is a good place to start.

* * *

There is a belief that the body is localized and physical and that it contains awareness. It is believed that the body is solid with a center where it can perceive the world, along with all its pleasure and pain. Also, it is additionally believed that the body contains the mind where the "I" as a creator functions from. There is a perception that the individual is born when the body is born, and that the individual dies when the body ceases to be. All these assumptions are the root cause for believing in duality and suffering.

* * *

The so-called body is arising in No-Thing-Ness as What-Is-Happening and is falsely labeled as the body. As soon as it is labeled, there is a sense of "mine" or of a personal body. The label causes the world of duality, and cause and effect is thusly born, and this state has to be experienced by the "worry-center" as a separate-self.

* * *

Even being aware of a body as a solid body is too much doing and no being.

* * *

Therefore, the definition of a body is as follows: No-Thing-Ness is seemingly the sensing of What-Is-Happening that is forming "It-Self" as sensory information, which is called bodily-sensation and appearing as a body.

* * *

No-Thing-Ness is not separate from sensing of What-Is-Happening, but apparently, the naming or labeling (an act of measurement) limits its free movement, and therefore the "worry-center", or a "me" is formed. The nature of "me" that is lack and fear is experienced by an individual as suffering.

* * *

Seemingly there is this body acts as a "center" being here and the world outside as an object. Apparently, the sensing of What-Is-Happening is happening by No-Thing-Ness, which has no center.

* * *

The belief in separation apparently causes the formation of divided thoughts, distorted bodily-sensation, and false perceptions; like what happens in a bad dream. Its projections are the appearance of the mind, body, and world, which are all arising and falling in the world of duality. waking up ends the personal story of an individual.

* * *

Memory is not a storage place of the past or future events which is located somewhere in the body. Memory is just a next thought that is framed and labeled by a memory, believing that there is a physical body. Memory-thought is what apparently is happening, and because of its nature being reactive, it gives an expression of an individual with a story having the past and future and, therefore, the memory of those events which force the next thought to arise and continue.

* * *

Memory is What-Is-Happening as a next memory-thought and is happening by no one and to no one.

* * *

Apparently, existence itself is continuously going in and out of existence, like waves of the ocean.

* * *

When No-thing-Ness is forming, it is the sensing of What-Is-Happening which is appearing as thinking, seeing, and hearing and when it is disappearing, it becomes the eternal potential.

* * *

Sensory information has no meaning and is impersonal. It is when an individual labels this nameless sensory information, and also the reaction that arises from the sub-conscious limits it and makes it personal. This personalized movement is appearing from a "center" as a doer or a thinker who believes in the duality of the world and so the cause and effect. To summarize:

Seemingly, the vibration of bodily-sensations is picked up by the ears and apparently interpreted as sound to be heard by no one.

Seemingly, the vibration of bodily-sensation is picked up by the eyes and apparently interpreted as sight to be seen by no one.

Seemingly, the vibration of bodily-sensation is picked up by the nose and apparently interpreted as smell to be smelled by no one.

Seemingly, the vibration of bodily-sensation is picked up by the skin and apparently interpreted as touch to be felt by no one.

Seemingly, the vibration of bodily-sensation is picked up by the mouth and apparently interpreted as taste to be tasted by no one.

* * *

When there is distortion in bodily-sensation, apparently it is called dis-ease. This distortion did not start at the level of the bodily-sensation but rather at the level of the sensing.

* * *

As soon as What-Is Happening is labeled and is identified as a personal event, the suffering starts for the individual which sees itself as separate from the event by judging it.

* * *

Animals and humans utilize the sensing of What-Is-Happening seemingly as a compass to navigate life. It is called instinct in animals and intuition in humans. What makes it different in humans is apparently a sense of self-actualization, which allows for separation from the totality of the Whole in avoiding pain in the hope of finding everlasting happiness. All of this is based on an illusion that there is a world separate from the "Self".

* * *

We have no access to the so-called physical world other than through the sensing of our senses.

* * *

Perception of the world through five sensory perceptions (Waking State):

VOID is prior to the essence of No-Thing-Ness with no movement at all.

The essence of No-Thing-Ness apparently is the sensing (knowing that it is being self-aware) of What-Is-Happening as sensory information/vibration named sight, projecting itself to appear as the sight, seeing, and being seen for no one.

The essence of No-Thing-Ness apparently is the sensing (knowing that is being self-aware) of What-Is-Happening as sensory information/vibration named touch, projecting itself to appear as touch, touching, and being touched for no one.

The essence of No-Thing-Ness apparently is the sensing (knowing that is being self-aware) of What-Is-Happening as sensory information/vibration named sound, projecting itself to appear as the sound, hearing and being heard for no one.

The essence of No-Thing-Ness is the sensing (knowing that is being self-aware) of What-Is-Happening as sensory information/vibration named aroma, projecting itself to appear as the aroma, smelling and being smelled for no one.

The essence of No-Thing-Ness is the sensing (knowing that is being self-aware) of What-Is-Happening as sensory information/vibration named taste/flavor, projecting itself to appear as the taste, tasting and being tasted for no one.

Perception of mind and body through three sensory vibrations (Dreaming State):

The void is prior to the essence of No-Thing-Ness with no movement at all.

The essence of No-Thing-Ness apparently is the sensing of What-Is-Happening as sensory information/vibration named bodily-sensation, projecting itself to appear as the bodily-sensation, being and being sensed for no one.

The essence of No-Thing-Ness apparently is the sensing (knowing that is self-aware) of What-Is-Happening as sensory information/vibration named thought, projecting itself to appear as thought, thinking and being reflected upon for no one.

Perception of No-Thing-Ness (Deep Sleep State):

When the sensing is being aware of sensing as being "Self-Aware", No-Thing-Ness is realized for no one.

* * *

No-Thing-Ness is apparently arising as "That". When the body and mind dissolve (dies), what remains is No-Thing-Ness.

* * *

It is a false assumption that everything is solid. Solidity is actually the dance of "Empty-Ness" for no one.

* * *

When an individual remembers an event in the past or the future, it is not actually an event that happened, but rather it is the No-Thing-Ness as the sensing of What-Is-Happening forming as sensory information/vibration of so-called thinking, remembering, or feeling; impersonal, for no one.

* * *

What an individual sees the world, is actually the sight as the appearance of the sensing of What-Is-Happening on the screen of No-Thing-Ness as being seen. For example, sensory information of sight apparently projected out into the world and perceived as seeing an object. There is nothing actually to perceive. There is only an illusion created by the five sensory perceptions of the world, along with the sensory vibrations of the mind and body that are being perceived as real; just like an image in the mirror that is not real, and it is only a reflection.

* * *

The so-called mind and body connection seemingly projects the movie of manifestation out into the world to be experienced by an individual as its story of "me". In reality, there is no "me" or even an individual. What-Is-Happening is all spontaneous arising and falling (appearing and disappearing) of phenomena in No-Thing-Ness as No-Thing-Ness, by No-Thing-Ness, and back to No-Thing-Ness. This is all impersonal. This state, which is free and liberated becomes a state of suffering when it becomes personal.

* * *

When there is no reaction to a feeling of fear, No-Thing-Ness, which is "Self-Aware" (sensing being aware of sensing), remedies the distortion based on the law of resonance. "That" which is being sensed but labeled as fear, apparently in the Now moment is being restored as love.

When there is no reaction to a feeling of lack, No-Thing-Ness which is "Self-Aware" (sensing being aware of sensing) remedies the distortion based on the law of resonance and "That" which is being sensed but labeled as lack, is apparently in the Now moment is being reinstated and restored as abundance.

When there is no reaction to a condition called dis-ease, No-Thing-Ness, which is "Self-Aware" (sensing being aware of sensing) remedies the distortion based on the law of resonance and "That" which is being sensed but labeled as dis-ease, apparently in the Now moment is being healed as well-being.

When there is no reaction to a condition called a sense of separation, No-Thing-Ness which is "Self-Aware" (sensing being aware of sensing) remedies the distortion based on the law of resonance and "That" which is being sensed but labeled as an individual or "me", apparently in the Now moment is being self-realized as No-Thing-Ness.

* * *

Fear is the contradiction or limitation that has been brought about by the sense of separation.

Lack is the contradiction or limitation that has been brought about by the sense of separation.

* * *

The "I" or the individual is in search of prosperity, health, wealth, passion, and purpose. What-Is-Happening is impersonal movements of so-called prosperity, well-being, wealth, love, and fulfillment, which is already "Is", but distorted by the desire of the individual, which is based on the deep-rooted feeling of fear and lack.

* * *

After realization, there is going to be subtle conditioning for the functionality of this so-called mind and body connection.

* * *

When there is light, there is no darkness. Darkness is resistance (backing away) from light. When there is Divine light, there is no separate-self that is present.

* * *

Separate-self, "I", or an individual, is a contradiction. Its nature is tightening. It is unease, and its so-called body is the reflection of this contraction, which lives in a state of uneasiness and stress. When the dis-alignment falls away, the body accordingly responds to that alignment by being healed. When full alignment seemingly happens, there is no longer cause and effect, ease or dis-ease, or bad or good. Instead, what is realized is the liberation and freedom that has always been in the background of What-Is-Happening. There is a final realization that "I", "me", or an individual never happened and the "worry-center" was really a shadow of No-Thing-Ness.

* * *

Conditioning or contradiction in the so-called body is sustained by the illusion of "I" or an individual. When separate-self falls away, the feedback loop is apparently broken, and constraint is realized. What-Is-Happening now has no individual or "I" to call it "my body", "my story", "my pain", and "my suffering". Everything is allowed to be "As-It-Is". The story of separation has fallen away, and there is a realization that the individual, or "I", never happened. After this realization, there should be enough self left for the sensing to sense through its sensors to function with no more center as "I" to sense the separation.

* * *

The harmonious actions that are formed by appearing and disappearing of No-Thing-Ness are the normal functioning of the so-called body, but the contradiction or resistance that is caused by a reaction to this neutral functioning because of believing in separation, is the cause of suffering.

* * *

When there is a reaction, the appearance of the false concept of the solid body appears, and it changes by the vibration of "What-Is". One moment it might be dis-ease and another moment, ease. This process is called spontaneous healing.

* * *

Body sensations apparently are happening, and the individual makes it personal by calling it "my body", which it becomes the "center" for "me" or a separate "I", or, an individual to operate from. To make the story even more fascinating, "me" adds more bells and whistles such as beliefs, habits, and behaviors to make it "my success story" or "my failures", while What-Is-Happening is a neutral process which is happening by no one and to no one.

* * *

The raw experience of this moment is colored and limited by the beliefs and memories of the "I", which creates a false sense of "me", a "center" which is called the body and its projection as the world. One of the most common feelings is the fear of a separation, which is buried in deepest layers of the body called the human psyche, and it is the last frontier for an individual to become aware of and to let go.

* * *

When the sensing of What-Is-Happening stops happening as the so-called mind, body, and the world, all that remains is the void of the concept of what it is called "my body". This is similar to an ocean; when its inner current stops whirlpooling, all that remains is the void of the concept of what it is called the ocean.

* * *

Naming a so-called emotion such as sadness or fear would prison the individual in the sense of separation, which sustains the belief system. This is, in fact, the cause of the deep-rooted sense of separation. At the end of all, is the need to drop all conditioning and letting the self-inflicted wound of duality to heal itself by the truth of "One-Ness".

* * *

When the so-called individual dissolves, its shadow falls away and disappears, as does its limitations. What remains is the light that comes from the realization of "True-Self", not as this or that, as a limited version, but as this and that as "Un-Limitless".

* * *

In the case of an individual, which is only a label for What-Is-Happening, it has no life to live. What-Is-Happening is spontaneously arising and falling, with no beginning and no end, with no meaning, no purpose, and it is being lived by no one. There is no individual who can ask why because everything is "What-Is", and the light of No-Thing-Ness is shining and embracing ALL as the sensing of What-Is-Happening.

* * *

Calling an emotion wonderful or awful does not limit its "Source", but instead limits the relationship of an "I" with the "Source". How pleasant or how terrible the experience of "me" is has a significant consequence for the individual but not for the "Source" because that all experiences are part of the totality of "All-There-Is". No-Thing-Ness is free from the so-called body which its nature is tension, and its feelings are about fear and lack.

* * *

The so-called "my body" as a solid entity with layers and layers of conditioning is just the limited interpretation of bodily-sensation. A core belief of something is wrong based on separation from its "Source" is the *feeling of pain and the sensing of suffering* in the body. At every moment, being ignorant of its true nature, the self wants to resist What-Is-Happening and control something which is "Un-Controllable".

* * *

The pain that the individual feels as "pain-body", followed by a sense of suffering and, therefore, a drama, and the individual calls that story "my life". The "pain-body" is the story of the separate-self hiding itself in the false notion of "my body", "my pain", "my world", and "my miserable life". All these layers of conditioning give more fuel to the momentum of separate-self, which likes to be hidden in an undeniable way and resists its dissolution. The feeling of pain and suffering apparently dissolve and disappear with an understanding that there is no individual or a doer such as "I", and what remains after this realization is What-Is-Happening as the sensing of "All-Is-Well".

* * *

The body is happening in no time, but apparently thought arises, and so the concept of the past and the future, along with many other perceptions based on deep conditioning and limitations, while everything is happening in "Boundless-Ness" and "Time-Less".

* * *

With an impersonal thought and impersonal feeling, there is the sensing of What-Is-Happening projected as a universal mind, body, and the world to be experienced by no one.

* * *

The individual apparently is longing for liberation and freedom, which comes about by the dissolution of the "me" or the individual. The nature of No-Thing-Ness is "Whole-Ness", (the force of non-duality is in action for dissolution of the idea of separation). The longing disappears when understanding turns into the realization that the "Realized-One" is never separate even for a second in the field of "Absolute-Being".

* * *

Still, there is a "center" apparently functioning from the point of view of a separate-self. The illusion continues with its play of cause-and-effect. The individual is self-sustained as more drama is unfolding, and the wheel of suffering continues to play its part to add more fuel in order for the concept of "my body" as an idea of separate-self to continue.

* * *

There is a notion that there is a path of spirituality for the entity to purify and to transform itself through the self-discovery that is going to happen in the future. While also on the path, the entity disappears like a shadow in the light of its own "Bright-Ness" by an unwavering force of grace.

* * *

Apparently, surrendering of the so-called mind is freedom from seeking enlightenment.

Apparently, surrendering of this so-called body is liberation from seeking health.

Apparently, surrendering of this so-called heart is liberation from seeking God.

* * *

A belief that "something is wrong", which comes from the sense of separation keeps the story of the individual as a victim alive.

* * *

The thought and, therefore, belief is believed to be the cause of suffering. The deepest suffering of all is the belief that is caused by layers of conditioning, which are interpreted as "I am separate from God". With this belief comes reaction, tension, and misery, which is still all are appearing and disappearing in No-Thing-Ness.

* * *

The so-called inward journey is not a physical action for finding the truth that is hidden somewhere in the body, waiting to be discovered. Rather like waking up from a dream, that there is not a material world outside of the self to be conquered or to wake up from a false concept of a solid body that is struggling to survive. With the realization of the "Source" as the sensing of What-Is-Happening comes the peace which transcends all understanding and with it, the disappearance of the mind, body, and the world as it is known by its false concept.

* * *

As long as the so-called body and mind are being fed with the story of "me", the drama carries on, apparently as the game of finding something that is not lost. When seeking ends, the false "me" drops with no trace, and the light of No-Thing-Ness illuminates ALL as the only light to dispel the shadow of duality.

* * *

Purification is the process that so-called mind and body goes through to cleanse itself of all the deep layers of false conditioning, memories, illusions, limiting beliefs, and to make the way to No-Thing-Ness as the "Form-Less", "Death-Less", and "Time-Less".

* * *

Individual self always acts with its limited movement; therefore, it cannot realize "That", which is "Limit-Less".

Individual self always acts with its lack of sincerity; therefore, it cannot realize "That", which is "Empty-Ness".

* * *

No-Thing-Ness is "All-There-Is", and nothing can be found outside of it as "me", or the "center", or an individual. The story of the individual seeking the truth of "That" is futile because "me" is What-Is-Happening within the field of "Absolute-Being" which is unrestricted and free from seeking the "One-Ness".

* * *

Anything that the individual, or "me" knows is based on assumption and limitation for the sake of communication. This labeling and framing have been going on for such a long time that nothing is close to its true nature in reality. As a result, the individual is living in a bubble of limitation, or better said, in a prison of its own restricted thoughts and beliefs in order to feel safe and secure. Apparently, there comes a time that "worry center" feels the pain and senses the suffering of being prisoned and dreams of a path of spirituality to liberation. The individual has thought and has found a path that can be walked on by reading, learning, and understanding to achieve the truth and freedom. Years go by before an individual realizes that never even for a moment has the "I" been separated from the peace and liberation that transcends all understandings. The individual realizes that its essence is "Pure-Knowing", "Pure-Awaring", and being "Self-Aware" and recognizes its substance is "Substance-Less". And "That" has always been shining without a second as No-Thing-Ness that knows "It-Self", as "It-Self", and by "It-Self" before it disappears back to "It-Self".

* * *

The body is an image in the mirror and cannot change its image by changing its reflection in the mirror. Knowing the body as the projection of No-Thing-Ness with no substance of its own and only as the essence of No-Thing-Ness is enough for the healing of separation to happen. Anytime the so-called body aligns itself with its "Source", which is called "Attunement", it is bringing itself back into harmony with its cause and the effect and self-healing happens effortlessly in "Time-Less".

* * *

Believing in space and time apparently projects a so-called "center" as mind and body. Therefore, its reflection in the mirror as "my body" is followed by a desire of an individual to get well as something that needs to happen in the future, while its essence is the sense of "Well-Being" that is not of time.

* * *

Before realization, conditioning such as labeling and judging, are happening all the time to allow for an individual to function. After realization and falling away of "me", "mine", "I", the sense of separate-self still functions and continues actions such as walking, talking, thinking and turning its head in response to a name call, *but there is no longer an individual, or an "I", who has a relationship with "What-Is"*. It is only What-Is-Happening with no meaning or purpose, which remains only as of the "Good-Ness", the "Easi-Ness" of No-Thing-Ness as "Pure-Being". Its essence as "Love", "Kind-Ness", and

"Tender-Ness", continues and apparently gives birth to a kinder, gentler mind and body toward the world.

* * *

When the so-called body is seemingly in-tune with What-Is-Happening, it is shining in joy and peace. This is the absence of believing in a personal thought as a separate-self that is keeping the light of truth from the "I", or an individual which is kept in the darkness of ignorance of separation.

* * *

When the concept of the body is formed, and it is believed to having a center with a sense of here and there, it relates itself being separate from the outside world, and this separation from other people and events causes judgments and, therefore, struggling and of suffering to follow.

* * *

Seeing and hearing a car passing by and knowing that it is only a projection is like seeing a body in the mirror and knowing absolutely that it is a reflection of an image. *What keeps the illusion of a body as real, is believing in thoughts that say otherwise.* Worse than thinking an image in the mirror as the real body is the belief that you can change the so-called reality (what-is) by changing its reflection in the mirror. In "Truth", there is nobody known as a body, no mirror, and therefore no reflection. It is all rather a play of light, with no purpose and no meaning other than just the sensing of What-Is-Happening as the essence of "One-Ness" that takes shapes of many different images as this and that and at the same time, not as this and that but "Pure-Being".

* * *

The individual knows itself to be a solid body, but not as No-Thing-Ness as the sensing of the bodily-sensation, which its reflection is the projection of a body.

* * *

There is an individual who is fighting dis-ease, while What-Is-Happening is the sensing of "All-Is-Well" and its essence is to heal "It-Self" from the false concept of division.

* * *

Individual, or "me", cannot change anyone or hold anyone responsible because there is nobody to change anybody or to put anyone at fault. What-Is-Happening is the goodness itself with nothing outside of itself to change.

* * *

The individual is liberating itself from the illusion of separation when it realizes that any seeking or searching for the "Truth" is the covering up of what it is looking for. Then and only then is the dissolution of "me" and returns of the individual back to "It-Self" in the way of the sensing of What-Is-Happening and back to No-Thing-Ness.

* * *

Individual, or "worry-center", resists or reacts to What-Is-Happening, which is the cause of Suffering. Meanwhile, when suffering is being seen in the light of understating, then what is realized is that What-Is-Happening, as the essence of No-Thing-Ness, which has no cause with no effect, therefore also has no action or reaction completely being at ease because its nature is "Non-Resistance" and "Easi-Ness".

* * *

The individual believes that to be a separate entity; it needs to change the effect, while the truth is that its essence is No-Thing-Ness, which is its own cause and effect, and there is nothing outside of itself to change.

* * *

Feelings of sadness and anger are just impersonal movements of No-Thing-Ness as emotions that are arising, just to dwindle back to "It-Self" so long as there is no resistance to its happening. The individual assumes by being the "center" and by making such a neutral process personal as good or bad, evil or virtuous, and right or wrong forces its own struggle in order to bring relief to the situation and therefore, results in suffering.

* * *

"All-There-Is" is the individualization of No-Thing-Ness apparently appearing as the mind and body, and also the world and its desires spontaneously are fulfilled by its own nature, which is "Desire-Less-Ness".

* * *

The so-called body that is apparently individualized is illuminated with the light of No-Thing-Ness and rejoices with "All-That-Is", as "Body-of-Nothingness" until it has disappeared back into No-Thing-Ness.

* * *

No-Thing-Ness is the sensing of What-Is-Happening and apparently its reflection and projection are as varying formulations or modulations of the original form. It is like the ocean appearing as a current to a wave to a drop of water – all sharing the same essence; "One-Essence" individualized in various forms.

* * *

There is not someone who is living an individual life, but rather What-Is-Happening is seemingly rejoicing from the essence of No-Thing-Ness in variation forms and different modulations as What-Is-Happening.

* * *

The "End-Less" or No-Thing-Ness apparently is constraining "It-Self" as the appearance of this so-called body or stone because it is "All-There-Is".

* * *

There is no need for an individual to figure out the reason or to struggle to survive because there is no one or no individual. "All-There-Is" is What-Is-Happening as the "Cause-Less".

* * *

The feeling of lack and fear are not physical and are the projections of an individual with an apparent center. When "me" dissolves, so does the lack, fear, perception of a body, and the world as it is known by the individual.

* * *

When "me" or individual disappears, so does the humanmade figure and concept of God.

* * *

"I", the mirror, and reflection of an individual in the mirror are all illusions. They are all illuminated holographic of No-Thing-Ness.

* * *

The individual as a body is not listening, but the listening is What-Is-Happening as illumination of No-Thing-Ness for nobody.

The individual as a body is not hearing, but the hearing is What-Is-Happening as illumination of No-Thing-Ness for nobody.

The individual as a body is not seeing, but the seeing is What-Is-Happening as illumination of No-Thing-Ness for nobody.

The individual as a body is not thinking, but thinking is What-Is-Happening and as illumination of No-Thing-Ness for nobody.

The individual as a body is not sensing the bodily-sensation, but sensing of bodily-sensation is What-Is-Happening as illumination of No-Thing-Ness for nobody.

The individual as a body is not seeking, but seeking is What-Is-Happening as illumination of No-Thing-Ness for nobody.

* * *

No-Thing-Ness is the sensing of What-Is-Happening as bodily-sensation illuminates itself as the appearance of a body.

* * *

The body is the illumination of the sensing of What-Is-Happing, projected onto the screen of No-Thing-Ness, by No-Thing-Ness, as No-Thing-Ness, back to No-Thing-Ness.

* * *

There is no mind and body but the sensing of What-Is-Happening as bodily-sensation and thought sensation

142

illuminated by the light of No-Thing-Ness seemingly projected onto the screen of No-Thing-Ness.

There is no external world, but the sensing of What-Is-Happening as five worldly sense perceptions illuminated by the light of No-Thing-Ness seemingly projected on the screen of No-Thing-Ness.

* * *

There is no dis-ease because there is no individual to have the disease. Dis-easing, which is the distortion of What-Is-Happening, is just happening and reaction, which is formed by the belief based on the duality of a "center" is forming the reality of dis-ease for "I", or the individual, to experience and suffer from.

* * *

What is being resisted or reacted upon apparently is becoming a reality, and the outcome of it, much like a shadow of ignorance, is covering or veiling the light of No-Thing-Ness.

* * *

What-Is-Happening as joy, peace, harmony, and well-being are all sharing the essence of No-Thing-Ness.

* * *

Seemingly after this body dies and so the perception of it as a solid body dissolves, so is the sensing of What-Is-Happening as the bodily-sensation and the illumination of the sensing of What-Is-Happening. What remains is no more story, no more drama, no more Karma. This is the dissolution of an individual or a separate-self as "I" and dissolving back into VOID, the eternal potential.

* * *

With every thought of pain and suffering when is not resisted rather embraced, God heals the sense of separation by the light of grace, which dispels darkness and restores "Full-Ness" and "Wholly-Ness" as love. Asking on the personal level for body to be healed brings momentary relief but reunion with the "One-Ness" is the ultimate relief from human suffering on the cosmic level.

* * *

Nobody is surrendering because the nature of "I", individual, or "worry-center" requires resistance. "Me" is the resistance to What-Is-Happening, and its struggle is felt as fear and lack by the individual who is living in a state of chaos.

* * *

There is no limitation or conditioning. They are all the movements of God. There is only the reaction to What-Is-Happening (it means having a reactive relationship to What-Is-Happening) that creates a sense of separation, and consequently, in the world of duality, a concept of an individual is born.

* * *

Being an individual as an observer to find the truth is the very act of veiling the "Truth".

* * *

The body seemingly is the name for the form that is happening spontaneously without any effort as the reflection of What-Is-Happing, which is illuminated by the pure light of No-Thing-Ness as "It-Self" and by "It-Self".

* * *

The false concept of a solid body does not mean that the body is not there, but rather a body is like the sea of vibration that is being interpreted and named as a solid body. It is the pure light of No-Thing-Ness, which, in its essence, is an absolute sense of well-being always "Being-At-Ease".

* * *

The body is apparently a form, illuminated by the pure light of No-Thing-Ness. The assumption by an individual, that to have a solid body as its "center" here and a world of reality out there, separate from this "Source", could affect the body's health when it is not at ease with "What-Is". In fact, the body is nothing but pure light of No-Thing-Ness reflected on the screen of No-Thing-Ness functioning harmonious and in-tune with "Easi-Ness," as the essence of well-being.

* * *

To make an attempt to make "me", a better "me", is like putting more labels over the dysfunctional "me" is useless, because "I" is just a label and any attempt for self-improvement is confirming the sense of separation. There is no "me", "mine", and "I" to begin with.

* * *

The dream is the collective experience that is happening in the mind of a dreamer who is dreaming different dreams at night and wakes up knowing that all was just a dream. Similarly, the realization of the "Truth" is just like the individual is waking up to the truth that there is no "I", "me", or "mine. There is only a play of light as sensing by No-Thing-Ness.

* * *

There is no individual who is seeing with an eye or tasting with a tongue. Seeing spontaneously is happening, and a thought followed by a belief is labeling the whole process by an "I" who is seeing. There is no eye that sees, no nose that smells, and no ear that hears. The seeing, hearing, touching, smelling, tasting are all spontaneously happening as What-Is-Happening.

* * *

Seeing is a phenomenon as What-is-Happening and not direct functionality of an eye that sees.

Hearing is a phenomenon as What-Is-Happening and not direct functionality of an ear that hears.

Tasting is a phenomenon as What-Is-Happening and not direct functionality of a tongue that tastes.

Smelling is a phenomenon as What-Is-Happening and not direct functionality of a nose that smells.

Touching is a phenomenon as What-is-Happening and not direct functionality of a skin that feels.

* * *

No-Thing-Ness is the sensing of What-Is-Happening as pure vibrations of love, and so:

Bodily-sensation as pure vibration of well-being.

Thought-sensation as pure vibrations of loving thought.

Ear-sensation as pure vibrations of joyful music.

Eye-sensation as pure vibration of blissful scenery.

All these impersonal sensations are arising and being perceived as part of the feeling, thinking, hearing, seeing, tasting, touching, and smelling— all projecting on the screen of No-Thing-Ness for no one.

* * *

Ignorance is the identification with a body as an individual or "I", which is separate from its "Source".

* * *

This identification with a body creates limitations such as lack and fear that is lived by the individual as pain and feeling of suffering. Only the "Un-Limited" is liberated to be nothing and everything all in the "Time-Less".

* * *

No-Thing-Ness is the sensing of What-Is-Happening as vibration/sensory-information of thought, which are forming/appearing as "Thinking", projected out-there on the screen of No-Thing-Ness. That is all part of how creation happens.

* * *

Pain is not a signal to become worried about dis-ease, but instead, it is an indication to come into alignment with the sensing of "All-Is-Well" and "Ease-Ness" of What-Is-Happening on a deeper level and surrendering to "That".

* * *

With the concept of a mind and body, comes a wrong belief about the world as being real. Without identification with a mind and body, there is only the "Is-Ness", "Is-Ness", and "Is-Ness".

* * *

When healing from dis-ease is apparently needed, "Ease-Ness" appears as What-Is-Happening until it is not, all spontaneously.

When a hearing is apparently needed, the sound appears as What-Is-Happening until it is not, all spontaneously.

When seeing is apparently needed, the sight appears as What-Is-Happening until it is not, all spontaneously.

When touching is apparently needed, the touch appears as What-Is-Happening until it is not, all spontaneously.

When tasting is apparently needed, taste appears as What-Is-Happening until it is not, all spontaneously.

When smelling is apparently needed, smell appears as What-Is-Happening until it is not, all spontaneously.

When thinking is apparently needed, thought appears as What-Is-Happening until it is not, all spontaneously.

* * *

Sound, sight, smell, touch, taste, though, and bodily-sensations are sensory information which are forming and appearing as hearing, seeing, smelling, touching, tasting, thinking, and feeling with an instrument called the body and mind. All are spontaneously arising and subsiding as "It-Self", by "It-Self", to "It-Self", back unto "It-Self".

* * *

The life of a so-called individual is all about maintaining and providing essentials for "I" to operate from, while there is nothing that actually exists as "I". "I" is the sensing of What-Is-Happening. Calling it "I", or an individual, gives the appearance of something that exists and needs to be sustained, and that takes effort. The "Source" of the apparent individual or the "worry-center" is No-Thing-Ness that is not in need of being continued or provided for as it is the "Source" of ALL creations. It is "Time-Less" and "Space-Less," and "empty-Ness" which is and also is not. Why bother!

* * *

When No-Thing-Ness apparently at birth identifies "It-Self" with five sensory perceptions as the world and two sensory sensations, such as mind and body, the sense of separation is born and so too ignorance. Identification entirely with the world, mind, and body gives a sense of a "center" that is in the body and mind and the world being out-there. The sense of separation stays with an individual throughout its life who is going to live as the "I" until it is not.

* * *

The feeling is forming when emotion which is neutral is intensified by the reaction at the level of the subconscious mind.

* * *

Identification with the body creates a sense of separation, and therefore, pain and suffering are born. It is not that God has turned His back on us, but we as individuals have turned our back to God, by accepting the concept of the body and mind and the world as real and No-Thing-Ness as a false reality.

* * *

Apparently in the real world, what is shown in the mirror is the reflection of mind and body, but in "Truth", there is no mind and body, nor the world as the individual knows it. All is the play of light of Self with "It-Self".

* * *

Life-force is the individualized movement of No-Thing-Ness as it arises and falls, which manifests the concept of mind and body as an individual with a "center" and apparently a real world. No-Thing-Ness is the stateless state that apparently is the subject and its projection as objects are appearing and disappearing without any distortion and therefore, there would be no world of cause and effect and Karma.

* * *

Reaction as a cause has to happen in order for its effect as the mind and body and the world to appear.

* * *

Sensing is the language of the inner world and the substance of creation. With the sensing of What-Is-Happening, apparently the creator is creating its creation as tasting, seeing, touching, hearing, smelling, thinking, and feeling, while at all the time, sensing is being aware of sensing as No-Thing-Ness.

CHAPTER 6

Questions and Answers

As the disturbance makes water become aware of itself, so are the inquiries that make the individual becomes aware of "It-Self"

Q Why are you giving seminars?

A: There is no one here who believes that the "I" knows something, and you as the listener does not. It is No-Thing-Ness as What-Is-Happening, and it is being transmitted through this so-called mind and body, or the character. At the same time, it is being picked up by itself apparently over there; over there is apparently by you. It is all one. There is nothing outside of the sensing of What-Is-Happening, which is aware of being "Self-Aware". What is happening can be labeled as giving a talk or having a discussion, but all it is, is the movement of No-Thing-Ness happening spontaneously here and there and nowhere.

Q: What is the most challenging part of this message?

A: The message that there is no individual, or "I", who is seeking the "Truth", or wants to be liberated perhaps is complicated to accept. The individual, or "worry-center", started this journey, or search in order to find a supreme power and to have control over the events of its life. One day, the "me" realizes "What-Is-Uncontrollable" cannot be controlled, and in trying to do so, more suffering is being experienced. When the individual realizes this truth, the "I" dissolves and what is realized is No-Thing-Ness as the pure essence of the sensing of What-Is-Happening as being purely "Self-Aware".

Q: What is longing?

A: There is no one who is longing. Longing is the act of grace that is drawing back the self to "It-Self" by embracing What-Is-Happening which is the act of unconditional love. There has never been any separation to justify longing, but perhaps the gravity of the Whole taking back pieces of itself to "It-Self" to become "One", fulfills the desire to know God. It is like the part of the ocean that is a wave that is apparently going in a different direction from itself and comes back to its 'Source", which is the ocean, by the force and gravity of the ocean. There is no need for longing because the individual is the

"Self" that is being pulled back to "It–Self" and by "It–Self" without any effort.

Q: Describe humility.

A: Humility is the moment of realization that there is no Individual, "me", "mine", and "I".

Q: Do we have free will?

A: Free will is the phenomenon that is seemingly happening in the world of duality. In the world of non-duality, there is no choice. What is happening at the moment is What-Is-Happening without an "I" who wants to experience a specific outcome. Free will is the act of an individual, or "I", who thinks there is someone who has a choice to make its life better than it is. This belief by itself distorts the very outcome that the individual is searching for. All there is, is the will of God as "All-There-Is", which is fulfilling its own desire by being "Desire-Less". The individual calls these events miracles that are happening all around.

Q: What is praying, and what should we pray to?

A: The intention of an individual who is praying to God is an old belief and comes from the sense of duality. It means there is a "worry-center" here as the individual and God who is superior and somewhere in the sky who is going to listen to "me" to get "me" specific desired outcome. The act comes from the belief that there is a God who is judgmental and is holding back what is good from its own creation. The most sincere prayers are not asking or begging for something, but to know "I-Am-That", the "Invisible-Source" that is illuminating the light that is dispelling the darkness of ignorance as the Divine. Knowing this truth and "Being," is the highest prayer for the goodness of humanity which is "It-Self".

Q: What is Karma?

A: Karma is a projection of the individual's mind who believes in right or wrong and peace or fight. Karma is the result of an individual who believes in the world of duality, and therefore, in cause and effect. The individual believes the "I" has to live its own destiny until the Karma exhausts itself in order for the realization to be realized as part of the transformation process. In the realization of No-Thing-Ness, Karma is not present, because, there is no individual as others to create any relationship in the form of a reaction with the self.

Q: Then, who suffers?

A: There is no act of suffering and no person who suffers, or by any situation that the individual is suffering from. There is only What-Is-Happening that is distorted by the reaction of an individual who thinks it has the power to control pain, and therefore, the feeling of heartache, loss, and fear that is being felt. As long as the individual identifies with the false concept of mind, body, and world, which is based on being ignorant of its true nature, the "I" continues to suffer. The "worry-center's" reaction to the illusionary projection is causing belief in separation, which is the root cause of suffering. Otherwise, there is not an individual or the world which is causing suffering. In other words, suffering does not exist and is only a projection of a confused and divided mind.

Q: How to eliminate suffering?

A: Suffering and the end of suffering are What-Is-Happening in No-Thing-Ness. Both phenomena are arising in No-Thing-Ness. What ends the sorrow is the realization of the "True-Self". At this point, suffering stops and "dissolves" for no one.

Q: What is the purpose of this message?

A: Questions come from the "worry-center", which wants to make sense of the "Un-Known" to make it known, in order to feel secure. There is no purpose or a reason to draw any questions from this type of talk. For example, dancing is happening, and when the dancer is lost in the motion of dancing, there is no entity who wants to know the reason for this beautiful movement, which is happening from the one moment to the next in such a harmony. It is just what is happening as What-Is-Happening from the position of the wave to particle and back to wave. The so-called individual is lost in the dance, and there is no "me" who wants to know the reason for these genuine movements. Dancing is happening; so is life. There is no reason but just to get lost and to become one with the wave movement of the "Self" through JOY.

Q: What are the obstacles to the realization of the "Self"?

A: Ignorance. Believing that there is an individual who is going to realize the "Self". Realization already "Is" and any seeking to find it is based on being ignorant about the "Truth". The sensing of What-Is-Happening, which is "Self-Aware", seemingly is the direct path to be on.

Q: How do I overcome mental habits?

A: Keeping an awareness not on the activities of the mind as thought which is powered by beliefs and memories but on the "Knowing" that there is no mind, nobody, and therefore no separation. This Knowing dispels the darkness of ignorance in order for the "Truth" to be realized and to dismantle and end repetitive mental habits.

Q: What are the ways for realization?

A: Primarily, questioning everything with the intention of going back to the "Source" and abiding where "Truth" is. Even this is not true because abiding is What-Is-Happening, and it is not something that the individual is going to practice.

Q: What can be practiced?

A: The sensing of What-Is-Happening in its purest form is the practice as "Being". This is as far as the individual can go. The rest is about to let go and let the grace of God pulls the sense of the separate-self in order for the "One-Ness" to be realized. Humility, devotion, and a sincere heart is needed to surrender to God's will.

Q: How long will it take for someone to get to this stage?

A: The ignorance is until it not. Inquiry into this question with the intention of going back to the "Source" and abide, is an act of God's grace.

Q: Is being mindful important?

A: An individual practicing mindfulness in the hope of realization is an obstacle but being mindful that comes from the earnestness with no attachment to the result is what takes the "I" back to the "Source". Any desire is an obstacle, including a desire for becoming the enlightened one.

Q: Is intellect helpful?

A: Being an intellectual is a burden for the mind on this path. The sensing of What-Is-Happening has nothing to do with the mind because it becomes reasoning. Rather, sensing of What-Is-Happening that is being "Self-Aware" is the practice that is beyond the mind.

Q: Does my realization helps others?

A: There are no others who are in need of help. There is no mind, body, or the world. Realization of No-Thing-Ness is "All-There-Is", and there is nothing outside of "Self". The thought of others being real is from the point of view of an "I", who believes in being a separate-self. Everything apparently exists in the world as the projection of the sensing of What-Is-Happening, which is illuminated by the light of No-Thing-Ness. This phenomenon is similar to thinking that what is projected on the screen of a movie is factual, which in fact, is just a projection of a frame of a film that creates a sense of a story. At the same time, the apparent individual or others is still the essence of No-Thing-Ness as the sensing of What-Is-Happening. The ego or self wants to make everything about itself, rather than the "Self" in order for its legacy to continue.

Q: What is time?

A: Society has named and labeled Now as time and has divided and labeled the idea of time further by calling it a day, week, month, and a year. This is for the purpose of communicating, but in reality, there is only the sensing of What-Is-Happening, which is the Now, and its projection apparently creates a concept of an individual which its nature is of time in order for the "worry-center" to make sense of its continuing story.

Q: What is an illusion?

A: There is nothing outside of No-Thing-Ness. When an individual believes in the sense of separation, then this belief establishes a center here and its projection as a real-world being out there. Therefore, the imaginary relationship between "worry-center" and the world projects itself seemingly as a reality for "I" to live in. So, the world is real when there is an individual who believes it to be so, and it is not when there is only No-Thing-Ness as the reality of ALL. To realize this truth is helpful for an "I" to be in touch with the sensing of What-Is-Happening, which is more immediate and more real than to start out being aware of the world, which is too personal and mental.

Q: How to become peaceful?

A: When a belief in being a separate-self end, "Peace-Fulness" is realized as peace. Until then, apparently there is a world of chaos for the false "I" to experiment with, which is the reflection of a divided mind. As long as the individual believes it has a body, a mind, and is searching for happiness and peace, the individual is going to suffer. Furthermore, any search for peace is more noise, and the seeker continues to look for what has been sought after. For example, when the cycle of desiring for peace ends, what starts is craving for its opposite, which gives momentum for this great disturbance and confusion to continue indefinitely. As long as the individual is identifying itself with the mind, body, and the world, the cycle of cause and effect will continue. What stops this cycle of agony and misery is the realization of one's own true nature as "Self", which is not peace or noise but instead is what peace and noise arise from as No-Thing-Ness.

Q: What about seeking pleasure?

A: An individual who seeks pleasure and avoids pain, still lives in a world of duality. The cycle of cause and effect gives birth to Karma. Karma is the force that creates the next sequence of causes and effects. And so, this drama of false concept of an "I" who is living life is going to continue. In order to stop this cycle, Karma needs to halt, and for this to happen, the realization of the state of non-duality is essential. With the realization of unity the individual dissolves, and so the world of duality (cause and effect), and the force of Karma which gives birth to the next cause and effect, dissolve as well.

Q: Are problems real?

A: Problems are mind-made. They arise from a reaction to What-Is-Happening as not being good enough. As long as there are judgments against What-Is-Happening, there are reactions and, therefore, more problems that arise from the restless mind, which the same restless and anxious mind is supposed to solve. When there is a realization that the problem and its solution are all arising in the field of No-Thing-Ness just (in no time) to fade away, then clarity will shine through the fog of misunderstanding. At that time, when there is no more invented mind, there will be no imaginary problem and no ideal solution. There is a belief and therefore, an assumption that there is life, there is death, there are problems, but all are What-Is-Happening. All these impersonal phenomena which are appearing and disappearing in the field of No-Thing-Ness are being illuminated by the light of "Pure-Knowing" in order NOT to solve a problem for an individual and instead to give clarity and insight to the ignorance that there is no individual separate from its "Source".

Q: What is surrender? What is the purpose of surrendering and how to surrender?

A: Surrender is the act of giving up any idea or philosophy relating to the search for enlightenment. Because of deep conditioning and beliefs that the individual has acquired throughout the years, it unconsciously reacts to the content of what is arising as thought, which is colored and formed by the memory. On the level of the subconscious mind, these reactions are happening unconsciously all the time. The individual is not aware of this process, and so the cause of distortion remains active into the next moment and so on. Surrendering at the level of mind and body has no use because it brings more self-importance to "worry-center", who is walking the path of spirituality in order to make this practice more purposeful, meaningful, and more goal-oriented. There is no path to something that is "Point-Less". When the individual, or "I", realize this truth, that its existence is the distortion and alteration of the "Truth" itself, and there is no one who is surrendering and nothing to surrender to, then there is only surrendering as What-Is-Happening. At this point, the whole process of searching and seeking stops and collapses. The individual dissolves and disappears back into No-Thing-Ness like it never existed and what remains in the field of No-Thing-Ness as the essence and substance of "All-There-Is".

Q: What is a thought?

A: Thought is what is arising as What-Is-Happening in the so-called mind of an individual who is *identifying* itself with a body, mind, and a world. Actually, thought is the representation of an individual or "worry-center". A thought is the "I" and not separate from the "I". As long as there is identification with a mind and body which is based on ignorance, there is a thought that is arising, and it is going to be reacted upon based on beliefs, patterns of conditioning, memories, and expectations. Even desiring to have better thought is another thought that acts as a reactive-thought. The arising and reaction create a vortex that is not going to stop on its own because its energy is the force of the false self that gives momentum to its next movement. Every so-called thought is arising from the energy of the last push and pull and gives oomph to the next one. The chattering mind wants to control everything and is not interested in becoming quiet because it knows by "Being" so, it will end, and death of the mind and body which are only concepts is the last thing the superficial mind wants. *Its existence is based on the constant push and pull against What-Is-Happening.* What stops this whirlpool of sorrow is the realization that thought itself in any shape, form, nature, and with any meaning (being positive or negative) is the distortion and the cause of the noise that apparently wants to stop. With this realization and deep understanding, thought and therefore the individual dissolves and what is realized is a reality with no opposite, which is the "One" as "Thought-Less", "Empty-Ness", "Change-Less", and "All-Pervading".

Q: What is ignorance?

A: Self-identification with a mind, body, and a world is ignorance of the "Truth".

Q: Describe the world?

There is no world that is separate from an individual. It is only a projection of an innocent misunderstanding. World, which has no existence of its own, cannot give the individual what it wants, because, at its core, it is not real and is only the projection of No-Thing-Ness as the sensing of What-Is-Happening. The world is seemingly a reflection that is reflecting its own reflection and being reflected back upon "It-Self'", by "It-Self", and through "It-Self".

Q: How can an individual become free of the feeling of lack and fear?

A: As long as the individual believes in the feelings of lack and fear and wants to get rid of it, resist it, or fill it with another pleasant feeling, results in suffering. This is because the search for fulfillment is the distortion and distraction itself, as well as the cause for sorrow. After realization, there is absolute clarity and conviction that the feelings of lack and fear, the search for love, and even the caused suffering are appearing and disappearing into No-Thing-Ness. Like in an ocean, everything is the ebb and flow that is seemingly arising from the ocean, so too everything is arising in the mind and heart of God as No-Thing-Ness, by No-Thing-Ness, and back unto No-Thing-Ness. The Divine embraces everything, while its essence is of no thing as "No-Thing".

Q: What about sacrifice?

A: Who is sacrificing? What is it sacrificing itself for? There is an individual that believes in sacrifice in order to reach a goal, and by trying too hard, the over-reaching done by the "me" puts the so-called goal in the further distance. Life is happening like a river, transforming itself from moment to moment, always moving forward by its nature. Any over-reaching is a disturbance to the natural flow of this mystery. Apparently, existence is varied in different expressions, but at its core, it is What-Is-Happening, and any reaction creates distortion to its "Love-Essence".

Q: How to stay in the state of equanimity?

A: Equanimity is not something that needs to be practiced but rather is just to "Be". At the core of it, equanimity is the state of knowing that there are no longer reactions and no longer any forces of positivity or negativity at work in order to create turbulence of wrongdoing or right-doing. This is beyond being compassionate because there is no one to be the compassionate one. There is only the sensing of the absolute allowing for what appears, and it knows itself as "What-Is" and it becomes as "What-Is" and it disappears as "What-Is".

Q: I am feeling lonely. What should I do?

A: Being alone is the state of being for the earnest-one who is seeking liberation. The falsehood of being isolated comes from deep conditioning that believes in identifying with this mind and body, which apparently needs protection from the world. As long as there is a sense of separation from the "Source," every individual life is a lonely life to live, no matter if the "worry-center" has a partner or is living in a community. The biggest of lies is that there is a superficial individual who thinks it has been left to manage life by itself and is responsible for everything. Even this belief is selfish and not selfless. The "I" has forgotten how to live in the nakedness of No-Thing-Ness, and the cure for its separation is the remembrance of what truly is its nature. True loneliness is having no inner-love to share with anyone. One might live alone, but the love that is being illuminated leaves no place for the sensing of loneliness. Another way to say it is that the whole universe is within its "Being". There is no sense of loss or lack, as "It's" existence is the existence of everything and does not exclude anyone, and it is including everything. In this state of realization that thrives in the joy of being, there is no room to be lonely but knowing that ALL is you and you are ALL.

Q: What is sin, and who sins?

A: The action resulting from an individual who believes in separation from its "Source" due to being ignorant of its true essence, is called sin. When ignorance is no longer, so too is a sin. The individual does not need to be saved from sin, because there is no "I" separate from its "Source-of-Being", which is "Fault-Less," "Holi-Ness" and is "All-There-Is" as "Good-Ness" and "Well-Being". Sin is just a thought that is commenting otherwise. There is no one being a sinner who needs to be saved, and seemingly, sin is the veiling that keeps the "Truth" at a distance. The sensing of What-Is-Happening in its purest form is the light that shines on the act of so-called sin and makes it become one with the "Righteous-Ness" and "Blame-Less". With this realization, comes the clarity that there is no more a sinner, the act of sin, or what it has been sinned upon and caused to happen. Everything comes to a halt. The feeling of being at fault (at the level of reasoning mind), which is based on a belief that the individual (the sinner) who is at fault and is separate from the "Source", transforms itself through the sensing of flawless and becomes one with "Fault-Less". The field is free of all concepts that thrive in the JOY of being. It is inexhaustible because there is no "next" since it is "Time-Less". In the end, "All-Is-Well" is liberated from the concept of duality of being sinful, and therefore its cause and effect, which is called Karma.

Q: Is the longing for enlightenment an effective and practical path to realization?

A: The individual apparently is longing for liberation and freedom, which in reality is looking for "It-Self". In fact, liberation is disappearing into the idea of an individual who is longing. The nature of No-Thing-Ness is "Whole-Ness". The force of non-duality is apparently is an action that is taking place to dissolve the idea of separation and not the individual who believes in separation. The individual and its longing disappear when its sense of separation fades away in the realization of the "Realized-One". What remains is the knowledge that there is no separation even for a second from Divine. The way back to the realization of No-Thing-Ness is not through any actions, as saintly as this might be, but is the sensing as *earnestness* and unconditional love for the "Absolute-Being".

Q: Is putting in an effort needed to reach enlightenment?

A: A seed becomes a tree without any effort. The seed is the sensing of What-Is-Happening, which apparently is, at its core is the seeing of an earnest-heart, which is placed in the core of the self to evolve and remember what has forgotten. Any desire, effort, and struggle is the cause for the veiling of the truth of the enlightenment which is so obvious in its nature. The nature of the effort is based on an individual who is putting forth an action to get a specific result that comes from self-centered activities and for a selfish reason, whatever the reason might be. There is no individual who is putting forth an effort. Seeking and searching are What-Is-Happening, which is arising seemingly from the field of No-Thing-Ness, which is the sensing of What-Is-Happening. No-Thing-Ness sincerely desires to find "It-Self". Any distortion of this ordinary process that is expected to happen manifests itself as the apparent "worry-center", which is seeking and searching for something that was NEVER lost. If only this neutral process, which is happening anyway in a most harmonious manner, is left alone to be sensed by the silenced heart (which is labeled as having faith.), then what is hidden becomes obvious as the Now, which is beyond the mind as time and body as the space, and which is the "Source" that gives birth to time and space. "That" becomes realized as "Time-Less", and "Space-Less", effortlessly, of its accord. What remains is No-Thing-Ness being self-aware of the pure "Self-Aware-One" as the Divine.

Q: Who is perceiving?

A: There is no perceiver, perceived, or perceiving. The perceiver, perceived, and perceiving are all appearing and disappearing as What-Is-Happening, spontaneously with no gap. The individual divides and labels what happened (What happened is only a concept and a label by the mind related to What-Is-Happening in order to create time and space for the false concept of the mind and body to continue) to make sense of something that is "Sense-

Less". The process of limiting "What-Is", which is love, compassion, wisdom, and harmony, causes distortion and disharmony. Conflict and tension are arising as a thought of confusion and bondage and manifests its presence as the false concept of "worry-center", whose nature is based on the feelings of lack and fear. For an individual to control what is called destiny, the "I" divides and analyzes and justify What-Is-Happening to get its power back. When a thought understands (understanding is What-Is-Happening too) that it is only an agent for superficial changes, and that by its self-centered actions, it cannot realize the real which is "Change-Less" and "Self-Less", then it stops and goes back to the heart as love-thought by the act of surrendering (surrendering is What-Is-Happening too). Clarity of this understanding brings about total surrendering to "What-Is", which ends in the realization of "One-Ness".

Q: How and why are we suffering?

A: Ignorance, and therefore suffering, arises when a neutral sensation is labeled and reacted upon by identification with a body, mind, and a world. An individual suffers when it gets stuck with beliefs, concepts of good and bad memories, and expectations. At the same time, beliefs, memories, expectations, and the individual are all apparently happening in the field of No-Thing-Ness. This understating dissolves the idea of duality and therefore suffering. Like the movie on the TV screen, the images in the movie, the light, the story, the screen that shows the film, and layers of complexity of the relationships, all are being projected as one story to be experienced. If any elements are separated from the rest, the meaning is lost, and the same is with the world of non-duality. Nothing is separate from God as it is all Godlike and Divine and free and liberated "As-Is". With the realization of this truth, ignorance of separation disappears, and so does the individual like it never existed. Therefore, suffering is gone as if it never happened and "Joy-Full" is realized.

Q: What is death?

A: Death is a made-up expression that has to live up to its expectation as being the biggest fear of all. Its opposite is birth, and what is born as a false concept of body has to end (die). But both death and dying, and birth and living are all What-Is-Happing in the vastness and emptiness of No-Thing-Ness. Nothing can separate these moments as there are no starts and no ends to them. It is just what is happening. By letting "It" just be like the flow of the river as it is, with no start or end, not getting stuck on the banks of the river, the flow of life with no resistance, it will run its course as "It-Is". There is nothing special about "It"; it has no name, no personality, no belief, no expectations, no color, and no shape. *The mere sensing of What-Is-Happening brings the essence of "It" into so-called existence, and the mere sensing of What-Is-Happening ends the essence of "It" out of so-called existence. Similar to a mature leaf, when its time comes, it falls without a story.*

Q: What is the world?

A: World is the appearance of the sensing of What-Is-Happening. It is not real because it is changing in relation to what is happening based on beliefs, memories, and desires of "I". The world does not have any substance of its own, just like an image in the mirror. It cannot give the restless individual what it wants because it is the projection of the inner world of the individual itself. The world of impersonal is arising and falling away and changing in the mind of God. It is appearing and disappearing in No-Thing-Ness. The individual labels everything to keep fear at a distance. Sensation, emotion, feeling, me, I, world, mine, you, yours are imaginary concepts, created in order to make sense of what is happening, but in reality, all is one, and one is all. When an individual deeply desires what is and does not want what is not, the "worry-center" dissolves, and so does the world imagined in a way that makes the individual know it as a fearful place to live in. The world loses its effect and power on an individual because, after waking up, something so real becomes part of a dream. All that remains is the "I-Am-Ness" as Now, which appears and disappears spontaneously on the screen of No-Thing-Ness without any relationship with an individual. Still, the sensing of What-Is-Happening is happening without any separation between the observer, what is being observed as the world, and the act of observing because they are all "One" in their totality in the mind of God. What is connecting all is unconditional love and harmony. When the ever-changing dream that once was imagined to be "my life" is over, so the concepts of my body, mind, and the world disappear, and what remains is No-Thing-Ness as the "Absolute-Being".

Q: What is the memory?

A: Memory is not a storage place for what has happened in the past, or what could happen in the future. It is not a location somewhere in the body. Memory is just a next thought that is framed and labeled as a specific piece of information that seems to be true until it is questioned. There is a belief that there is a body that is physical and lives in time and space and has the past and future. A thought that is colored by memory as a memory-thought is what apparently is happening. Because of a reaction by the memory, which causes push and pulls based on "should" or "should not", a memory gives an expression of an individual with a desire for pleasure and avoiding pain. This action and reaction causes more stories of the past and future and, therefore, further memories of those events, like a vicious cycle that never ends. By realizing the structure and nature of thought, the memory of an individual based on "should" or "should not" disappears like a patient who is put to sleep for surgery and does not remember anything about the operation after recovery. So too, is the individual who has lived a life with all its drama and stories. Apparently knowing that What-Is-Happening is meaningless (the way individual thinks) or hopeless is liberating because the truth of it, is taking away the urge of being hopeful, eager, ambitious, and motivated. All of these goals are the driving force of an individual, or "worry-center" to continue, and when they fade away,

"I" no longer is. At the same time, there is no longer a process of thinking that is comparing What-Is-Happening to the memory of what has happened to make a continuous story for the doer. The memory, which is operating on the subconscious level, which is the illusionary warehouse of ideal imaginations, expectations, hopes, opportunities, anticipations, habits, goals, desired images, fearful images is no longer, and "What-Is" stands alone. "What-Is" is liberated and unconditionally fulfilled in real-time as the No-Thing-Ness and as the "Illuminated-Self" with no memory of the past and no expectation for the future. It is happening as the sensing of What-Is-Happening, in Now.

Q: Who is the observer, and what is the object of observation?

A: The observer, what is being observed, and the act of observing are all "One", appearing and disappearing in No-Thing-Ness. Seemingly, the mere sensing of What-Is-Happening gives birth to the impression of mind, body, and the world with no one in the role of the observer. The No-Thing-Ness in one breath denies every thought, every feeling, every word, and every action as "No-Thingness". In the next breath, it embraces every thought, every feeling, every word, every action as being "All-There-Is". That is the meaning of coming and going out of existence. When "Infinite" emerges and appears as "Finite", and the world appears, then "Finite" disappears back into its source and becomes "Infinite," and the world disappears.

Q: What are the Awake State, the state of Dreaming, and the state of Deep Sleep?

Perception of the World — Awake State

Sensing is not happening as the individual knows the meaning of happening. In other words, sensing is "Move-Less" and always "Self-Aware" that gives the impression of the world, similar to an awake state.

No-Thing-Ness is apparently the sensing of What-Is-Happening that is forming as sensory information or vibration called touch and appearing (which is being "Self-Aware") as touching for no one.

No-Thing-Ness is apparently the sensing of What-Is-Happening that is forming as sensory information or vibration called sight and appearing (which is "Self-Aware") as seeing for no one.

No-Thing-Ness is apparently the sensing of What-Is-Happening that is forming as sensory information or vibration called sound and appearing (which is "Self-Aware") as hearing for no one.

No-Thing-Ness is apparently the sensing of What-Is-Happening that is forming as sensory information or vibration called aroma and appearing (which is "Self-Aware") as smelling for no one.

No-Thing-Ness is apparently the sensing of What-Is-Happening that is forming as sensory information or vibration called taste and appearing (which is "Self-Aware") as tasting for no one.

Perception of the Body and Mind – State of Dreaming

Sensing is not happening as the individual knows the meaning of happening. In other words, sensing is "Move-Less" and always "Self-Aware" that gives the impression of the mind and body, similar to a state of dreaming.

No-Thing-Ness is apparently the sensing of What-Is-Happening that is forming as sensory information or vibration called bodily-sensations and appearing (which is "Self-Aware") as being for no one.

No-Thing-Ness is apparently the sensing of What-Is-Happening that is forming as sensory information or vibration called thought and appearing (which is "Self-Aware") as thinking for no one.

No-Thing-Ness – The State of Deep Sleep

Sensing is not happening as the individual knows the meaning of happening. In other words, sensing is "Move-Less" and always "Self-Aware" that gives the impression of no world, similar to a state of deep sleep.

No-Thing-Ness is self-aware as being present as an Absolute.

Q: Who is the individual, and what is its reality?

A: An individual is a thought that is arising due to the force of memories which are continuously reacting to "What-Is". The *individual is a thought* that is identifying itself with a body, a mind, and the world. It has no substance of its own, and its essence is changing based on the content and nature of the memories, which are just illusionary imaginations, expectations, hopes, opportunities, anticipations, habits, goals, desired, and fearful images. The "worry-center" appears as the sense of separation and continues its activities in the field of pain and sorrow, always desiring happiness. Even though the essence of an "I" is the joy; it is still in pursuit of happiness. And when the individual wakes up from false identification with the body and mind, just like from a dream, it dissolves in "Non-Existence" and so does its imaginary world, like it never existed. What remains is not an "I" as a person. Only the sensing remains, which is not related to an individual but is instead the sense of the "Self" that is integrated and merged into the sensing itself.

Q: What is the root of cause and effect?

A: While cause and effect are happening in the world of duality, there is no cause and effect in the state of non-duality. In a state of no resistance, everything happens spontaneously without anything to be called an object or a subject. This neutral happening eliminates the arising of cause and effect because of not having any relationship with itself. The distortions, which are the reason for the presence of the state of duality are born out of reaction, and as long as there are ignorance and identification with a mind, body, and the world, the cycle of Karma is kept going. There would only be an individual as a separate-self who lives in the burden of sorrow. The sensing of What-Is-Happening spontaneously arises because there is no "worry-center" to cause it. Divine is "I", and "I-Am" is the cause for its own illumination on the screen appearing as "I-Am-Ness". It is its own causation, which is radiating as itself, by itself, through itself. No-Thing-Ness, which is the background of the sensing, is the light that has no substance and is "Cause-Less". It is the cause for its own illumination, and it is the light that shines through all the pictures and images on the screen, which are appearing and disappearing spontaneously by the movement of this phenomenon which is leaving no trace behind. It is labeled as God

Q: Who is the sincere devotee?

A: Divine is the devotee, so too the acting of the devotion, and the devotion itself. And so are the lover, the act of loving, and the beloved. When it is left-alone to "It-Self", it is pure absolute, and it is dancing the dance of love and devotion. Its movement has the essence of love and dedication to itself, by itself and through itself and there is nothing outside of itself to take ownership of it as the devotee. Its essence is the supreme compassion that glues everything together. While the apparent outer chaos is going on, "It" is embracing everything, even the innocent act of ignorance that comes from the individual who is forgetting about not being "The-Only-One", as "Its-Own-Self".

Q: Why is desire denied?

A: The deep meaning of the desire for something comes from a hidden feeling of lack and fear, which establishes the individual's desire for what-is-not and also explains it's running away from what-is. This vicious cycle never ends. Desire does not exist by itself. *By the intention of avoiding pain, desire is born, and by the intention of wanting pleasure, desire is born.* Consequently, after years of craving and aversion, the habits, beliefs, condition, hopes (however glorious), self-imposed ideas, and memories, are all expended in the pursuit of happiness. Whatever has a beginning has to have an end. Apparently, there comes a time that nothing makes the "worry-me" happy, and therefore chasing desire stops when the cycle runs its course. What happens to be very clear is that nothing has been lost at any given moment. Seemingly, racing from one pleasure to the next is the sensing of What-Is-Happening on the blank background of the screen of No-Thing-Ness. The individual with all its desires, habits, conditions, and personal memories dissolves, and what remains is No-Thing-Ness effortlessly fulfilling its desire for "It-Self", while being the "Desire-Less-One".

Q: Explain more about "I", "I-Am", and "I-Am-Ness".
A: The following metaphor is beneficial:
"I" is the potential and possibility of becoming a tree. It is the ever-present knowledge that is hidden in the seed. (The creative potential that arises in No-Thing-Ness).

"I-Am" is the seed that becomes a tree. (The projection of creativity on the screen of No-Thing-Ness).

"I-Am-Ness" is the tree, which has the essence of the seed and its knowledge. (The creation itself formed by No-Thing-Ness).

As the "I-Am-Ness", as What-Is-Happening disappears, the "I-Am" is realized, and when the "I-Am" disappears as the sensing of being aware of being "Self-Aware," the eternal "I", is realized as "Just-Is-Ness". It is the so-called space that makes the perception of the mind, body, and the world to come to existence and disappear unto.

Q: What gives the impression that this world is real?

A: Continuity gives the expression that this world is real and is born out of an association with time and space. Time being made out of the projection of the mind (memory- thought that compares its content to the past and the future) and space is the projection of the body with the sense of here and there, that arises and appears; all are a dream in the mind of God. If there is no associative memory or identification with a mind and body, or time and space, objectivity and subjectivity end in the "Time-Less" and "Space-Less". What remains is the ever-present in the eternal Now, without any continuity in time and space. It is the "Absolute-Being" that gives expression and impression to everything while it is No-Thing-Ness.

Q: Do we need to practice detachment in order to find happiness in realizing God?

A: Who is going to practice detachment? There might be a desire for detachment for the sake of seeking God, but that desire is also what is arising in the field of No-Thing-Ness. There is no getting away from not being one with the "One-Ness" of all. There is an idea of detachment, but it is What-Is-Happening that is colored by the essence of unconditional love. There is no individual who needs to practice detachment. There is a so-called concern, or worry, which arises from the "worry-center" and which wants to put the effort in to end its attachment to the world. However, in the field of duality, what arises is distortion. Because at the center of it, there is an individual that is trying endlessly to detach itself from suffering in the hope for realization. Even detachment from self in order to realize God is an attachment. Attachment and detachment are all happening in the field of No-Thing-Ness. It is like a dog running in tight circles endlessly to chase its own tail. It is laughable when the dog is doing the act, but it causes suffering for an individual who is trying so hard to pursue happiness hopelessly. When there is finally a realization that there is no "me", "mine", or an "I", apparently the movie called "in pursuit of happiness" stops. There would be nothing more evident than metaphorically walking out of the movie theater for good. When we wake up from the dream world, all sins, concepts, dramas, expectations, beliefs, opinions, thoughts, attachments, detachments, hopes, devotions, faiths, and desires, all as false concepts drop off and what shines through is love, by being "Just-Isness".

Q: Describe what time is.

A: Individual or worry-center is confusing the tick-tock of a clock connected to eternal "Change-Less". While the tick-tock of a clock is external, and its purpose is for "me" to function, the internal clock is the "Ever-Changing" and "Change-Less", which is appearing and disappearing in different forms as "Form-Less".

Q: Is the realization requires an individual to become aware of God?

A: No-Thing-Ness, which is the same name for God, Divine, "Absolute-Being", and "One-Ness", is realized already. There is no individual who needs to realize the "One-Ness". "One-Ness" is all there is. In the world of duality, the practice of abiding, attaining, or surrendering is required by an individual to realize the "One-Ness", but not in the state of non-duality. God is God with seeking or without seeking. It is "What-Is", and it is appearing and disappearing, leaving no trace or reason to be found when it has never been lost. Self-forgetfulness is the story that the individual has about the Divine and not the other way around. Meanwhile, practices such as attaining, surrendering, striving, and letting go, abiding and denying, forgetting and remembering, are all What-Is-Happening, which are all also the expression of the

Divine. "Just-Isness" is self-fulfilled, as it is spontaneously arising, only to subside in the vast ocean of No-Thing-Ness. All that remains is this, its essence of bliss, "In-Joy" with "It-Self", as "It-Self", back unto "It-Self", with no purpose or concept, as the "Realized-One".

Q: What about love?

A: Love is. Love is about being and not about doing. The divided and confused mind of an individual has a misperception about what love is.

Love is not to get or to give. Love "Is".
Love is not to express or impress. Love "Is".
Love is not about indulging or restraining. Love "Is".
Love is not to give or to receive. Love "Is".
Love is not passion or hate. Love "Is".
Love is not needy or over-reaching. Love "Is".
Love is not in the future, past, or forever. Love "Is".
Love is not being honest or dishonest. Love "Is".
Love is not the highest or lowest virtue. Love "Is".
Love is not fear or lack. Love "Is".
Love is not petty or open-minded. Love "Is".
Love is not about winning or losing. Love "Is".
Love is not to desire or to deny. Love "Is".
Love is not to be displayed. Love "Is".
Love is not vulnerable or invulnerable. Love "Is".
Love is Now.

Q: What is death, and who dies?

A: True death is the ending of an illusion of separation. An individual gives importance and value to a block of time called the period of "my life" which starts with birth and ends in the death of the individual, but along the way, in every so-called moment, there is birth and death as vital as the first and the last one. Death is seemingly painful because it is viewed and labeled by the distorted and limited mind as a final event with no return into the unknown that causes grief. It is not dying or death, but an idea about it that is causing sorrow. When an individual dissolves, and so makes the mind, death loses its importance and becomes a natural transition that is happening in every moment. What is arising and fading away, and appearing and vanishing, and coming into sensing and going out of sensing is What-Is-Happening in a form which apparently has a beginning and an end quite spontaneously without any purpose or destiny, story or drama. What is coming into existence as "New" is going to die in order to make space for the next "New". What is coming into being as a new breath has to make room for the next breath otherwise the organism suffocates. It is like a wave in the ocean without any beginning or an end, like ebb and flow, emerging and subsiding. The ending of one wave is the beginning for the next wave; inseparable. Waves are coming in and going out of existence without any waves that are attributed to the precious or the worthless one. And as the sensing comes to an end, naturally, what remains is void of everything as the VOID, which has no beginning and no end, being the eternal potential.

Q: What about responsibility?

A: In the world of cause and effect, responsibility apparently is necessary for an individual to live by, but in the state of non-duality, there is no notion of guilt or responsibility because there is no individual who is in charge. What is arising is being met by specific action of fulfillment as What-Is-Happening. Existence without fear and desire looks like living life effortlessly, like a free-fall with no one literally being in control. So, there is a responsibility or not, but it all depends on whether the "worry-center" is or is not.

Q: What is existence?

A: Pulsation and expansion of No-Thing-Ness as No-Thing-Ness, by No-Thing-Ness, are all called existence. Its presence is called life-force and individualized as e-motion. An individual associates this natural rhythm, which is pulsating and forming and de-forming, as a physical body, mind, world, life, karma, time, space, now, destiny, happiness, enlightenment, and misery. The wonder is that No-Thing-Ness that is changing and being changeless, as the compassionate one embraces and forms "It-Self" based on what is being associated with because it is the "Almighty-One", "Merciful-One", and the "Loving-One".

Q: What is the concept?

A: The concept is a make-believe memory-thought which justifies itself to ease the pain of separation. It is the warehouse of patterns, beliefs, labels as the good, virtual, god, selfish-love, virtue, trust, bad, right, wrong, success, failure, purpose, destiny, sorrow, and hope. It labels the "Truth" with something that is known in order to make sense of it, and in the process of associating and identification, it distorts the actual "Truth". There is no concept of an "I" or "me" in the "Truth", and that is what an individual is afraid of. It is fearful of all of its investment as being an individual when the concept of the individual falls away and is left literally with nothing. There is nothing for "me" to figure out because there is no individual in charge or in control, and when there is no self, the "Self-Less" is realized. Abandoning all notions and thoughts is apparently called the process of purification and transformation, which is What-Is-Happening in the silence of pure, attentive, sincere, and earnest heart. In truth, all there is "Just-Isness", pure "As-Is", naked as "Unconditional-Love", which is always, purely in love with "What-Is" without any hope, attachment, detachment, desire, or destiny. So simple!

Q: Is God love?

A: God is not love but emanates the perfume of love endlessly by way of expanding and extending. At its core, the "Self-Less" essence is pure light and love; therefore, "It" is free to be the lover, beloved, and to be the loving one. It shines on just and unjust, sinner or saint. It is "Just-Isness" with no name, ceaselessly embracing everything because nothing is out of "It-Self". "It" is the light that brings every form into the light of existence to shine, while it stays in the background of no dimension as an emptiness to call back to itself what is formless. It is the "Meaning-Less" that gives meaning to everything and the "Emotion-Less" that gives rise to e-motion. It is the "End-Less" that gives life and death and "Un-Conditional" that gives resistance a reason to continue. "It" is the sound for the deaf-ear, light to the blind-eye, a cure for a sick, a lift to the burden that is the body, clarity to a confused mind, a taste for the tasteless, and it brings order to chaos. "It" is the "Innocent-One" that loves the sinner and saint, powerful and powerless one. "It" embraces the precious and useless, flawless, and imperfect one. "It" is Omnipresent, Omnipotent, and Omniscient and is sensing the appearance that appears and ends within "It-Self" without being blemished. Being the "Un-Caused", which is independent of birth and death, "It" effortlessly, spontaneously, and in a heartbeat, gives a breath of life and in another takes the last breath back to itself, and returning to the VOID as causeless which is the cause of eternal potential

Q: Who are you?

A: I am What-Is-Happening. I am a message, messenger, and the act of messaging in the so-called field of No-Thing-Ness. There is no purpose, planning, and no specific lesson or practice that is being given here. There is no perceiver, perception, or perceiving. What is being expressed goes back to its source, as there is no object like the one who is giving a message and a subject who is receiving it. Nothing is done by anybody as there is no doer, thinker, or planner. There is no expectation since no one is here to receive. It is What-Is-Happening, and deeper than that, it is the sensing of What-Is-Happening. Even deeper is the sensing that for eternity being "Self-Aware". And at its core, there is No-Thing-Ness that is the message and the messenger and the act of communicating the message that is happening without any purpose and without the guarantee of getting any results. The realization is due to the sensing of What-Is-Happening, and there is not an individual who gets it or becomes an enlightened one. Hearing is happening, seeing is happening, thinking is happening, coming to the talk is happening, going home is happening, and so too, is disappointment and joy. All exist in the so-called field of No-Thing-Ness. No-Thing-Ness is the path and the individual who is walking on the path, and so also, it is the destination. There is no way out of it, since "It-Is-Everything". "Truth" is evident to the one who is earnest and sincere enough to stop wandering in the world of concepts, including searching for an ultimate God. There is no "me', "mine", and "I"; in this state-less state. Everything is as what-is happening and what-is not happening in Now, in the field of "All-There-Is".

Q: Who is the self?

A: Self, "me", "worry-center", "I", or an individual, are not entities. Self is a concept that comes to life from projection of a thought that is arising, powered by memories, expectations, habits, beliefs, fears, patterns of conditions, and then disappears just to continue in the next cycle. The existence of an individual is powered by the reaction to what-is that is caused by ignorance. Identification with the body, mind, and the world gives force to this sequence of events. This momentum of the cause and effect that is manifested by nothing that is turning the wheel of pain and suffering, also called Maya, will continue with its manifestation. This movie called "my life", seemingly will go on year after year on the screen of No-Thing-Ness with no end to its sorrow in sight except by realizing the truth behind the self as "Self". The self cannot realize "Self", because it is the very distortion which comes from labeling that limits the "Limit-Less" and that hides the "Truth". Self is the bundle of the past and future memories and is made out of hope, desire, and fear that conflicts with the nature of "It-Self". When a self gives up all the ideas and concepts about itself and ceases to be, then "Self" is realized effortlessly. Understanding this truth dissolves the seeker called the self or the individual into the "Empty-Ness", which is the eternal source. The essence of "Self", which is the nameless and formless, is the pure light that is shining endlessly to bring everything to the existence, in order to take it back into No-Thing-Ness, with no purpose as the individual wants to believes it.

Q: What is bliss?
A: Bliss apparently is the state that is:

The end of storytelling about an individual believing in separation and realization of "One-Ness" as "All-There-Is".

The end of projecting and believing in the world being out-there and realizing that the world is within.

The end of resisting what-is and being at peace with what-is not.

The end of being in control and being the "Power-Less", where power comes from.

The end of naming what-is and being the "Name-Less".

The end of letting go of finding purpose and being the "Aim-Less".

The end of pretending everything matters and being the "Matter-Less".

The end of struggling and being the "Effort-Less-Ness".

The end of creating chaos and being the absolute "Clarity".

The end of searching for self-protection and being the "Non-Resistance".

The end of being selfish and being the "Self-Less".

Q: What is the cycle of pain and pleasure?

A: pain and pleasure are dependent on each other. What this means is that desire for pleasure, for something that is not (what-is-not) is causing a distortion of What-Is-Happening, which causes pain and suffering. At the same time desire for not having pain (something other than what-is), is causing more distortion of What-Is-Happening, which causes more pain and suffering. Either way, desire is the root cause of pain and suffering; all based on "What-Is" which "Is" is not good enough. The individual may superficially create a state of pleasure by acquiring something, or by getting relief from pain, but these temporary states are not going to last. Every action that is coming from the notion of What-Is-Happening not being good enough is giving way back to the distorted version of What-Is-Happening, which is followed by pain and suffering. The leading cause of suffering is memory-thought that reacts by desiring what-is-not and avoiding what-is, which arises from the sense of separation that an individual apparently is associating with. Repeatedly the individual thinks life is happening to "I", and that "I" has to struggle or search for happiness and peace. *This universal false assumption that what-is, is not good enough, which is born out of ignorance, causes the world to be burdened by profound sorrow with no end.* It is like a glamorous object shining in front of the seeker who is always in pursuit of happiness to find ever-lasting love with no end in sight. This cruel cycle (only from the viewpoint of an individual) will go on as long as the individual believes that there is a body, mind and that the world is real until there is a deep understating that there is no separate individual who is seeking for pleasure and avoiding pain. The unified cause that is enforcing this momentum of Karma, as mentioned before, is the ignorance of the true nature of "What-Is". "What-Is" is "Just-Isness" and "Good-Ness" without any assumption. What is manifested in the world of the duality of cause and effect, by its law, has to continue its existence until the state of non-duality is realized, which is free from cause and effect and, therefore, also free from Karma. The so-called pain and pleasure, not-pain and not-pleasure, are spontaneously appearing, and disappearing from the field of No-Thing-Ness. It is the "Cause-Less", "Change-Less", "Form-Less", and "Flaw-Less" and it is the so-called Divine love that includes everything and excludes nothing because its nature is nothing everything and nothing. The No-Thing-Ness is never changing and ever-changing in its spontaneous movements as making love to "it-Self" out of nothing.

Q: What is conditioned, and what is not?

A: The body, mind, and the world, by their nature, are conditioned and are arising, forming, appearing, and disappearing from No-Thing-Ness and back unto No-Thing-Ness. Understanding this allows for liberation from the sensation called thought and from sensation called bodily-sensation, which they project the concept of the body, mind, and world. The dissolution of an individual is liberation from all concepts and is the realization of what is already realized as the "One-Ness". All is left to "It-Self" is, to be "It-Self", through "It-Self", and back unto "It-Self". In a way, nothing needs to be done because there is no doer. It is What-Is-Happening fulfilled "As-It-Is". Nothing is being judged or named because nothing is outside of "It-Self". Even the arising of a so-called thought, reaction, and manifestation is all What-Is-Happening, and all are in the field of No-Thing-Ness as the world, mind, and body. What is conditioned is "Unconditioned-One". There is no observer, observation, or what is being observed. What is arising and falling away, gives the impression of an observer but it is only a sensation which is the sensing of What-Is-Happening, apparently in the field of No-Thing-Ness. Not perceiving outside of the world and knowing where the illumination is illuminating from, is a leap from was is defined to "Un-Defined".

Q: Is there any choice to make?

A: Choice is just a concept. There is a notion of making a choice, but who is making a choice? The idea of having a choice is born from the sensing of resistance to What-Is-Happening, which causes restlessness. What-Is-Happening, which in its nature is not wrong or right but neutral, is arising as a natural phenomenon but a thought highjack what is arising and creates distortion by judging the Now. Because the nature of thought is conditioned, it takes the ownership of what is unconditioned and colors it based on its memory, conditions, beliefs, habits, expectations, and hopes of what it could have been or should have not been. Through this process, the individual blames, or takes ownership and announces the victory or failure for the outcome; a process that absolutely had nothing to do with the individual. Even choosing to be happy and peaceful is not a real choice because the resistance to "What-Is" is going to result in feeling more miserable and conflicted. There is no place for "should" or "must-not" because whatever is happening in the state of duality ends in division and limitation of what-is. Identification with a body, mind, and the world gives birth to a false concept of the individual who believes to have a choice, which is an addiction or pattern of conditioning that was established in early so-called childhood. There is a false idea of choice, but the true choice is in the background as the "Choice-Less" where there is no "me". What-Is-Happening is happening without any outside interference, but rather what arises as What-Is-Happening comes from one source and goes back to the same source, spontaneously and without any external interference because what is inside and outside are sensations spontaneously appearing and disappearing in No-Thing-Ness. This is the peace that the "I" is seeking for which with its searching hides the "Reality", which is peace. "Reality" is the silence that is always "Is", and is free from the disturbance, distortion, attachment, and detachment of an individual having expectations. "Reality" is the presence and absence of what-is through which, what-is, and what-is-not are all appearing and disappearing, having no choice but "Just-To-Be". The manifestation goes as such:

From "I" to, "I-Am", to "I-Am-Ness".

VOID goes beyond, merges into No-Thing-Ness, and comes across...

No-Thing-Ness goes beyond, merges into "Absolute-Being" and comes across...

"Absolute-Being" goes beyond, merges into the sensing of being "Self-Aware", and comes across...

The sensing of being "Self-Aware" goes beyond, merges into being aware of the essence of unconditional love as its core essence and comes across...

Being aware of the essence of unconditional love goes beyond, merges into the sensing of What-Is-Happening and comes across...

The sensing of What-Is-Happening goes beyond, merges into projecting "It-Self" on the screen of No-Thing-Ness that gives the creation and appearance of body, mind, and the world and comes across...

The appearance of the body, mind, and world goes beyond, merges back into VOID, and comes across...

And, there is a pulsation from VOID back to VOID, a rhythm of bliss, that can last an instant, a lifetime, or eternity.

Q: Is there a destiny?

A: Destiny is another false concept. Another name or a label to give meaning to the "Meaning-Less", "Point-Less", and "Empty-Ness" that is not of time and space. What an individual is hoping to achieve is the goal of fulfilling its destiny in order to give purpose and importance to its so-called life. *The individual is a player in a movie, and whatever choices that are being made, which are based on the assumption of separation is still being played on the screen of No-Thing-Ness. The realization of "What-Is" is the "Is-Ness" dissolving the notion of a separate individual.* All along the "Reality" is the light that is projecting the movie and its characters. At the same time, the screen that is absolutely blank, empty, and not filled with any concepts, is what the movie is being played on, which gives continuity to the story. Nothing is separate from another part in order to set a goal to accomplish a goal outside of itself. What-Is-Happening is its own purpose and does not need an individual that, as a matter of fact, does not exist, to give it direction. The sensing of What-Is-Happening is direction-less. It comes from No-Thing-Ness and goes back to No-Thing-Ness just to "Be". The No-Thing-Ness is its own source, which is of no time and no space with no destiny. When all the concepts, beliefs, memories, expectations, hopes, habits, patterns of conditions fall away, so does the continuity, and with it, what is real is effortlessly revealed as the "Reality", empty of all concepts. The hardest part is for the imaginary individual to wake up from the dream of storytelling and to realize the reality of "What-Is", "As-Is", free of all imaginations and desires.

Q: What is ego?

A: Ego is a manmade concept. It is a label on a character as its image that has no reality. It is a mere naming and a definition that is born from a sense of separation and identification with a body, mind, and the world. The self-image, which is a distorted idea as the ego, is going to be sensed until the individual dissolves, and so does its character. The ego keeps the "I" in the dark prison of duality. A seeker that is lost in the world of thoughts and formulations is being told to kill the ego in search of the "Truth". How can the ego that is a false concept and a mere name be destroyed? How can a shadow that has no reality and substance of its own be demolished? These notions blind the seer from seeing the "Reality". Only the light of "Truth" is what melts away what is false as self-importance and brings what is real to the forefront. Dropping and letting go of ego is another belief that is taking years for the seeker who is practicing spirituality to recognize. Rejecting what-is causes more chaos, more labeling and allows for the setting of more ambitious goals for the ego to chase and therefore justifying by being on the path of spirituality to reach enlightenment. And at the end, with no ambition, and with insight, it is realized that there is no individual whose ego needs to be destroyed in order to find enlightenment. If there is any practice, perhaps being sincere by and in the sensing of What-Is-Happening, which in its nature is made of clarity, purity, and integrity. All of this is illuminating the path of "New-Ness" to the unity of "One-Ness".

Q: Explain more about e-motion, sensing, and feeling. (updated version—selected essays from chapter 1)

A: The feeling is forming when emotion is intensified by the reaction from the subconscious mind.

The feeling is the sensing of the intensified emotion.

Reaction to emotion apparently arises from the deepest level of the subconscious mind as a feeling of anxiety, and as it increases, consequently, the emotion intensifies too through the cycle of actions and reactions, which is felt as fear on the level of mind and body. Meanwhile, the feeling of fear and anxiety is being embraced by the "Self" through love and compassion by the sensing of What-Is-Happening as "All-Is-Well". When there is no longer false observation to distort the sensing of What-Is-Happening by the five worldly sense perceptions and two bodily and mind sense perceptions, then there is a realization that the sensing is being aware of sensing (awareness is being aware of being awareness) in its purest state. What is clearly being seen is that No-Thing-Ness, like the pulsation of God, is running through all creations as the "Sense-Less," "State-Less," and "Form-Less" through which all sensing of the forms are seemingly appearing and disappearing. No-Thing-Ness is illuminating the illusion of body, mind, and the world as "It-Self," by "It-Self," to "It-Self" and back unto "It-Self".

Emotions are arising, being distorted by the mind and being felt like the feelings of anxiety, sadness, anger, and can even manifest as the feeling of bliss and happiness, private and personal in relationship to an individual. Framing and labeling through believing in separate-self is what creates a reaction to What-Is-Happening (which is impersonal) and creates the "center" that eventually starts reacting to emotion (which is impersonal) and forms the feeling of suffering.

There is nothing outside of emotions to make them personal. It is an impersonal phenomenon appearing and disappearing as What-Is-Happening.

No-Thing-Ness is the sensing of What-Is-Happening as sensory information of sight, touch, sound, smell, taste, bodily-sensation, and thought. These seven elements are forming and appearing as touching, hearing, smelling, tasting, being, and thinking. The emotion which is the subtle vibration of existence is being intensified by reactions that are caused by beliefs, memory, and limited conditioning, and therefore, feelings are being felt at the level of mind, body, and the world perception as the feeling of fear and loss. These intense emotions are being experienced by the individual and therefore, the reincarnation of these forceful emotions will continue appearing in the next moment called Now.

There would be no sense of separation if there is no more reaction which means the "I" or individual is dissolved, and love which is the essence of No-Thing-

Ness as subtlest emotion is being sensed in its purest form in the Now as the sensing being "Self-Aware".

Emotions are intensified by reactions on the level of the subconscious mind. These reactions are caused by identification with a mind and body. These intensified emotions are felt as feelings such as anger or hate by an individual who believes themselves to have these feelings. When the individual dissolves, what is left is the pure essence of What-Is-Happening in the form of love, peace, and compassion, which runs through all experiences for no one. For example, the bodily-sensation called back pain, which is What-Is-Happening, is continued by way of identification to the body, and therefore neutral emotions are now being intensified and being sensed (felt) as the feelings of anxiety, anger, and despair. As a reaction to pain becomes less and less, the emotions return to their neutral state and are sensed as their true essence of No-Thing-Ness, which is the sensing of "Well-Being". This process is called healing.

The neutral emotions are intensified to reactions (at the subconscious level) by the arising of seeing, touching, hearing, smelling, tasting, thinking, and being. These apparently heightened emotions are now called feelings and have reincarnated themselves every moment and become personalized feelings in a relationship with an individual. They are therefore being sensed (felt) as the feelings which an individual feels such as anger or sadness. Reincarnation is the label that is given to the next emotion and therefore feeling, that manifests itself as the personal feeling of an individual.

World perception is about sound, sight, taste, touch, and taste, which are forming as hearing, seeing, smelling, touching, and tasting as What-Is-Happening. Body perception is about bodily-sensation forming as being and mind is about thought to form as thinking. The effect of world sense perceptions and body-mind sense perceptions on neutral emotions are feelings which are being sensed and felt on the level of mind and body as the feeling of happiness or sadness. The sensing of neutral and impersonal emotions as the pure essence is the next subtle level, and the sensing of being aware of sensing (being self-aware) is the deepest level of sensing; the quickest way to the realization of "One-Ness".

Emotions are the movements of life-force and the activities of "Is-Ness" or No-Thing-Ness, which are giving form to the arising and subsiding of What-Is-Happening. Sensing, which is being self-aware, becomes the manifestation of No-Thing-Ness when No-Thing-Ness starts pulsing, which means it comes into existence. With the sensing of emotions as they are arising, the world comes into existence, and as it is subsiding, the world goes out of existence. This phenomenon is like the rhythm of God's heart beating as love.

The feeling is the reaction (the feeling is a reaction to the flow of life-force) to the emotion at the subconscious level by the so-called mind, which gives birth or manifests more intensified emotion as the feeling of suffering or anxiety. Reaction to emotion manifests the sense of separation that is called an individual or separate-self or "me". This is the vicious cycle of Maya (for Maya's definition, please refer to Q/A section), but the truth of a matter is that at all times, it is No-Thing-Ness as What-Is-Happening and not a moment separate from "That". As the false concept of mind and body drops away, so is reaction weakened, and the feeling of suffering softens. The sensing becomes more subtle and becomes more notable until sensing, which is being self-aware, is sensing the essence of No-Thing-Ness as pure unconditional love. Apparently, in the next state, as grace arises, the sensing that is being aware is abiding in the state of "Non-State" as "Un-Movable," "Time-Less," "Matter-Less," "Change-Less," and "Bound-Less" as "Absolute-Being". Without any sensation as the results of the dissolution of body and mind, then VOID "Is" as eternal potential.

Sensing appears and disappears in No-Thing-Ness. The sensing is the ripple of first or subtlest movement of No-Thing-Ness as pure unconditional love. As emotion intensifies to the reaction of the sub-conscious mind, then it is named or labeled as the personal feeling of an individual as the feeling of anger or happiness which is felt on the level of mind and body.

Emotion, when intensified, becomes feeling, and feeling is further reinforced by the reaction from the subconscious mind. They are all different names for the same "Source" they are arising from.

Sensing appears and disappears in the No-Thing-Ness. When it appears, sensing is the essence of No-Thing-ness as unconditional love, and when it disappears, VOID "Is", which is eternal potential.

To make this clear, the sensing is running through all the different apparent stages and appearances. Sensing of unconditional love embraces the feeling of What-is-Happening, such as the feeling of anger or anxiety. Also, No-Thing-Ness is not something that the individual can abide within, so everything permanently is part of No-Thing-Ness, including the "me" or the "worry-center". The individual gets stuck on the path of spirituality, believing that being an observer or someone who is being aware is the way to realization. No-Thing-Ness is "Just-Isness". That is all. It is not a container or a field that something is arising from. It arises as itself, by itself, and returns to itself. As long as there is any kind of movement, such as life-force, then there is sensing to be sensed. Another way to say this is that sensing is being aware of the sensing, which is not separate from God, and it is God that is "Self-Aware". Divine's nature is Omnipotent, Omnipresent, and Omniscient, and when there is no movement, GOD is void of any activities.

Sensing is self-aware of appearing and disappearing of what can be called life-force as emotions. As the sensing becomes pure in its purest form without any distortion from false-self, then it becomes aware of "It-Self" as No-Thing-Ness.

Emotion is seemingly arising. It is What-Is-Happening in its purest form, which is being sensed as love and apparently manifesting as feeling and being felt by an individual as fear by the power of reaction, based on ignorance.

Calling an emotion wonderful or awful does not limit its "Source", but instead limits the relationship of an "I" with the "Source". How pleasant or how terrible the experience of "me" is has a significant consequence for the individual but not for the "Source" because that all experiences are part of the totality of "All-There-Is". No-Thing-Ness is free from the so-called body which its nature is tension, and its feelings are about fear and lack.

Q: What is Maya?

A: Acorn, the seed of the oak tree has all the knowledge to become a huge oak tree, so does the seed of the unborn child have all the knowledge to evolve and become a being. The seed of the unborn child has the awareness from the past to any so-called future events. Also, it has the knowledge of the non-duality of No-Thing-Ness, and the truth of being the "One" void of all concepts, beliefs, patterns of conditioning. It has the knowledge of the illusionary world of mirage that is operating and influencing the individual during its lifetime. Ignorance of the fact that the individual is the "One-Ness", and that it is not separate from "One-Ness", along with identifying with the mind, body and world affairs, is what feeds the power that keeps spinning the wheel of suffering and so too, the continuity of the existence of what is called Maya which comes from believing in the world of duality.

Maya's own force generates more power to give momentum to turn itself and create more suffering. Resisting this power by wanting to stop it, adds more fuel to its motion of turning, and so it manifests itself seemingly every moment by the power that is inherent in itself.

cycle of Maya or suffering arises as a form, lasts momentarily, and then fades away unto itself. This is called birth and death that happens in each moment of a lifetime. This energy is just enough to generate the force that gives rise to the next instance of What-Is-Happening, and therefore, the cycle of suffering will continue with remarkable simplicity but profound suffering from this breath or the next, and from this life to the next lifetime. Apparently, something stops Maya to be seen indeed as what is, which is a false concept, wrong belief, and a made-up idea that an individual who was believed to be true. Profound realization of what Maya is, and its dissolution opens doors to freedom and the possibility of liberation.

What stops the wheel of suffering might be a tremendous sorrow, maturity of the so-called seeker, fearless and sincere longing to know "Truth", absolute realization of the false nature of "I" which is born out of action and reaction which disappears in grace of God. All these occurrences serve as the wrench that stops the wheel of Maya from turning forward and which reverse and ends the momentum of generating more suffering.

As a result, there comes the reverse process, from being in the world to going back to be the sensing of What-Is-Happening, going back to being "Self-Aware," and back to the "Source" of "All-Being". From being mesmerized by the glimmering of the world back to No-Thing-Ness is the cause of the dissolution of the world of Maya, which is called transformation and complete dismantling of an individual. Apparently, this so-called evolution of consciousness may happen over a short period or a long time, but the "force" is always there to call back part of itself as what is lost to where it belongs, back to its essence as "Just-Isness".

Q: More about the mind, body and the world (updated version— selected essays from chapter 5)

A: Body, mind, and the world are illuminated by the light, love, and in the image of God and not to be ill-treated by the divided and limited mind. A concept of the mind is born by the expression of a thought, and a thought arises by the continuity of memory of fear, which is based on believing in separation from its "Source". A thought that denies the unity of everything which comes from ignorance is the cause of conflict and suffering. A deep understanding of this truth is self-realization, which ends the burden of sorrow.

The mind is the projection of the sensing of What-Is-Happening on the screen of No-Thing-Ness, which is self-aware of itself as being "Self-Aware". The divided mind appears as a thought and, so too the world of duality and the concept of the body and when it disappears, so too the world of duality and the concept of the body and world, meanwhile, these reflections are happening only as an idea in the mind of God.

The finite, infinite, or absolute are all labels that are given to "That", the No-Thing-Ness, or God, by the mind. So how can the mind understand "That"? The mind as a substance that is living in time and space cannot understand the nature of No-Thing-Ness because its movement is always in the so-called past and the future. The mind cannot get, find, seek, or search for something that is "Time-Less" and "Space-Less". The very act of wanting to understand, get, or seek apparently puts the veil over the so-called "Truth" (Truth is a label too) and at the same time, the individual is seemingly a separate-self which is not separate from the totality of the Whole.

Apparently, the limited and finite mind which reflects and projects a body with the feelings of lack and fear is not separate from What-Is-Happening. In the time of realization, the so-called finite mind is dissolving back into the "Mind-Of-God" as What-Is-Happening, and what is realized is the sensing of love, compassion, and well-being.

Apparently, the finite-mind as a separate entity is the extension or instrument that "Infinite-Mind" of God as

"It-Self" is using to project itself in the form of the world, mind, and the body on the screen of No-Thing-Ness.

The mind and body are just labels. In fact, they are the so-called sensing instruments (sensory) that are sensing "It-Self" as what is being sensed. When the sensor, sensing, and what is being sensed dissolve in non-duality, what is realized is the "One-Ness" of "All-There-Is".

Sensing of I AM THAT I AM is the end of seeking. When "I" realizes that there is no individual, fear, and desire, which are the grossest form of vibrations which are on the level of mind and body fall away, and self is realized as the "Self".

By the use of the five world sense perceptions and two body and mind sense perceptions, life-force gives birth to forms by arising and falling in which What-Is-Happening comes to apparent manifestation as the illusion of world, mind, and body and disappears back to its "Source" where everything comes from.

There is enough conditioning of the individual by external elements that when an individual is being called, apparently, the individual turns its face and answers. There is seemingly enough conditioning left for the apparent mind and body to function in the world, while "All-Is-Happening" for no individual.

As the sunlight shines through water drops to make a rainbow, so does No-Thing-Ness illuminate various forms to reflect on the screen of God's Mind the "Uni-Verse" as "One-Song" in harmony.

Apparently, after birth, No-Thing-Ness identifies "It-Self" with two sense perceptions of the mind and body to manifest the concept of an individual and with five sense perceptions to perceive the world by that individual. Identification entirely with the world, mind, and body gives a sense of a "center" being as a mind and body and perception of the world out-there. The sense of separation stays with an individual throughout its lifetime as being a separate entity until it is not.

When so-called realization happens, the body or mind does not wake up, but the "Alive-Ness" becomes self-aware, which is always "Self-Aware" but it is hidden under the assumption of a belief that someone is waking up. "Truth" is so simple and obvious, and yet it is veiled by the seeker, and therefore, it is hidden.

Every mind and body has its own unique pattern and layers of conditioning. Seemingly, when it is being illuminated by the light of No-Thing-Ness, like the musical beat of the song, is expressing "It-Self" as intense energy of light as a different spectrum of love as a "Being". These vibrations are the harmonic rhythm of life and the vitality that comes from the "Source".

There is a belief that the body is localized and physical and that it contains awareness. It is believed that the body is solid with a center where it can perceive the world, along with all its pleasure and pain. Also, it is additionally believed that the body contains the mind where the "I" as a creator functions from. There is a perception that the individual is born when the body is born, and that the individual dies when the body ceases to be. All these assumptions are the root cause for believing in duality and suffering.

No-Thing-Ness is apparently arising as "That". When the body and mind dissolve (dies), what remains is No-Thing-Ness.

The so-called mind and body connection seemingly projects the movie of manifestation out into the world to be experienced by an individual as its story of "me". In reality, there is no "me" or even an individual. What-Is-Happening is all spontaneous arising and falling (appearing and disappearing) of phenomena in No-Thing-Ness as No-Thing-Ness, by No-Thing-Ness, and back to No-Thing-Ness. This is all impersonal. This state, which is free and liberated, becomes a state of suffering when it becomes personal.

After realization, there is going to be subtle conditioning for the functionality of this so-called mind and body connection.

As long as the so-called body and mind are being fed with the story of "me", the drama carries on, apparently as the game of finding something that is not lost. When seeking ends, the false "me" drops with no trace, and the light of No-Thing-Ness illuminates ALL as the only light to dispel the shadow of duality.

Purification is the process that so-called mind and body goes through to cleanse itself of all the deep layers of false conditioning, memories, illusions, limiting beliefs, and to make the way to No-Thing-Ness as the "Form-Less", "Death-Less", and "Time-Less".

Believing in space and time apparently projects a so-called "center" as mind and body. Therefore, its reflection in the mirror as "my body" is followed by a desire of an individual to get well as something that needs to happen in the future, while its essence is the sense of "Well-Being" that is not of time.

"All-There-Is" is No-Thing-Ness apparently appearing as the mind and body, and also the world and its desires spontaneously are fulfilled by its own nature, which is "Desire-Less-Ness".

www.ingramcontent.com/pod-product-compliance
Lightning Source LLC
Chambersburg PA
CBHW021358090426
42742CB00009B/907